FINDING THE LOST
IMAGES OF GOD

UNCOVER THE ANCIENT CULTURE, DISCOVER HIDDEN MEANINGS.

D1112067

Ancient CONTEXT
Ancient FAITH

FINDING THE LOST IMAGES OF GOD

UNCOVER THE ANCIENT CULTURE, DISCOVER HIDDEN MEANINGS.

TIM LANIAK

GARY M. BURGE: General Editor

ZONDERVAN®

ZONDERVAN.com/
AUTHORTRACKER
follow your favorite authors

ZONDERVAN

Finding the Lost Images of God
Copyright © 2012 by Tim Laniak

This title is also available as a Zondervan ebook. Visit www.zondervan.com/ebooks.

This title is also available in a Zondervan audio edition. Visit www.zondervan.fm.

Requests for information should be addressed to:

Zondervan, *Grand Rapids, Michigan 49530*

Library of Congress Cataloging-in-Publication Data

Laniak, Timothy S.
     Finding the lost images of God / Timothy S. Laniak.
        p. cm. (Ancient context, ancient faith)
     Includes bibliographical references.
     ISBN 978-0-310-32474-4 (softcover)
     1. Image of God. 2. God (Christianity) I. Title.
  BT103.L36 2011
  231'.4—dc22
                                          2011007935

Cover design: Kirk DouPonce, DogEared Design
Interior design: Kirk DouPonce

Printed in China

11 12 13 14 15 16 17 18 /CTPS/ 20 19 18 17 16 15 14 13 12 11 10 9 8 7 6 5 4 3 2 1

Dedicated to the patrons of the Robert C. Cooley Center for the Study of Early Christianity at Gordon-Conwell Theological Seminary—Charlotte. Their passionate interest in the Christian faith continues to support our ongoing explorations among its biblical and historical foundations

CONTENTS

ANCIENT CONTEXT, ANCIENT FAITH

EVERY COMMUNITY of Christians throughout history has
framed its understanding of spiritual life within the context of
its own culture. Byzantine Christians living in the fifth century
and Puritan Christians living over a thousand years later used
the world in which they lived to work out the principles of Christian faith, life, and identity. The reflex to build house churches,
monastic communities, medieval cathedrals, steeple-graced and
village-centered churches, or auditoriums with theater seating
will always spring from the dominant cultural forces around us.

Even the way we understand "faith in Christ" is shaped to some
degree by these cultural forces. For instance, in the last three
hundred years, Christians in the Western world have abandoned
seeing faith as a chiefly communal exercise; that is not true in
Africa or Asia. Among the many endowments of the European
Enlightenment, individualism reigns supreme: Christian faith
is a personal, private endeavor. We prefer to say, "I have accepted
Christ," rather than define ourselves through a *community* that
follows Christ. Likewise (again, thanks to the Enlightenment),
we have elevated rationalism as a premier value. Among many
Christians faith is a construct of the mind, an effort at knowledge
gained through study, an assent to a set of theological propositions.
Sometimes even knowing *what you believe* trumps belief itself.

To be sure, many Christians today are challenging these Enlightenment assumptions and are seeking to chart a new path. Nevertheless, the new path charted is as much a by-product of modern cultural trends than anything else. For example, we live today in a highly therapeutic society. Even if we are unaware of the discipline of psychology, we are still being shaped by values it has brought to our culture over the last hundred years. Faith today has an emotional, feeling-centered basis. Worship is measured by the emotive responses and the heart. "Felt needs" of a congregation shape many sermons.

Therefore, defining Christian faith as a personal choice based on well-informed convictions and inspired by emotionally engaging worship is a formula for spiritual formation that may be natural to us—but it may have elements that are foreign to other Christians' experience in other cultures or other centuries. I imagine that fifth-century Christians would feel utterly lost in a modern church with its worship band and theater seating where lighting, sound, refreshments, and visual media are closely monitored. They might wonder if this *modern church* was chiefly indebted to the entertainment industry, like a tamed, baptized version of Rome's public arenas. They might also wonder how ten thousand people can gain any sense of shared life or community when each family comes and goes by car, lives long distances away, and barely recognizes the person sitting next to them.

THE ANCIENT LANDSCAPE

If it is true that *every* culture provides a framework in which the spiritual life is understood, the same must be said about the ancient world. The setting of Jesus and Paul in the Roman Empire was likewise shaped by cultural forces quite different than our own. And if we fail to understand these cultural forces, we will fail to understand many of the things Jesus and Paul taught.

This does not mean that the culture of the biblical world enjoys some sort of divine approval or endorsement. We do not need to imitate the biblical world in order to live a more biblical life. This was a culture that had its own preferences for dress, speech, diet, music, intellectual thought, religious expression, and personal identity. Their cultural values were no more significant than are our own. Modesty in antiquity was expressed in a way we may not understand. The arrangement of marriage partners would be foreign to our world of personal dating. Even how one prays (seated or standing, arms upraised or folded, aloud or silent) would have norms dictated by culture.

But if this is true — if cultural values are presupposed within every faithful community, both now and two thousand years ago — then the stories we read in the Bible may presuppose themes that are obscure to us. Moreover, when we read the Bible, we may misrepresent its message because we simply do not understand the cultural instincts of the first century. We live two thousand years distant; we live in the West, and the ancient Middle East is not native territory for us.

INTERPRETING FROM AFAR

This means we need to be cautious interpreters of the Bible. We need to be careful lest we presuppose that *our cultural instincts* are the same as those represented in the Bible. We need to be *culturally aware* of our own place in time — and we need to work to comprehend the cultural context of the Scriptures we wish to understand. Too often interpreters have lacked cultural awareness when reading the Scriptures. We have failed to recognize the gulf that exists between who we are today and the context of the Bible. We have forgotten that we read the Bible as foreigners, as visitors who have traveled not only to a new geography but a new century. We are literary tourists who are deeply in need of a guide.

The goal of this series is to be such a guide — to explore themes from the biblical world that are often misunderstood. In what sense, for instance, did the physical geography of Israel shape its people's sense of spirituality? How did the storytelling of Jesus presuppose cultural themes now lost to us? What celebrations did Jesus know intimately (such as a child's birth, a wedding, or a burial)? What agricultural or religious festivals did he attend? How did he use common images of labor or village life or social hierarchy when he taught? Did he use humor or allude to politics?

In many cases — just as in our world — the more delicate matters are handled indirectly, and it takes expert guidance to revisit their correct meaning. In a word, this series employs *cultural anthropology, archaeology, and contextual backgrounds* to open up new vistas for the Christian reader. And if the average reader suddenly sees a story or an idea in a new way, if a familiar passage is suddenly opened for new meaning and application, then this effort has succeeded.

This is the fifth book in the Ancient Context, Ancient Faith series. In previous books we explored how the biblical world within the Middle East shaped the spirituality of those who lived there. We examined the cultural landscape, the parables of Jesus, even encountered stories where Jesus transformed the lives of individuals. We then took a remarkable tour into the spirituality of some of the Middle East Christians in the centuries after Christ.

When I first came across Dr. Tim Laniak's splendid *While Shepherds Watch Their Flocks: Forty Daily Reflections on Biblical Leadership*, I knew that this was a man who understood the contextual significance of the Bible and how understanding them changes our interpretation of the Scriptures. Having lived and studied in the Middle East, Dr. Laniak's abilities as a culturally sensitive Bible scholar make him unusually suited to explore the major motifs for God in Scripture. Serving as Old Testament professor and dean at Gordon-Conwell Theological Seminary (Charlotte, NC), he has helped scores of students in a variety of ministry settings understand the everyday nature of God's revelation. He knows how to do the necessary spadework to uncover hidden meanings in the culture of antiquity, and he is willing and eager to bring those truths home to those who live in the church from day to day.

As you will see throughout the pages of this book, men and women in the ancient world framed their understanding of God by using metaphors and images that could be pulled from their world. And after three thousand years, these ideas have been lost to us. Or worse, we impose on these metaphors ideas that we think are familiar. *Shepherding in Iowa is not like shepherding in the ancient Middle East.* But once we unlock these ancient concepts, a new world of meaning and understanding is ours. And in this case, Dr. Laniak will be our guide.

Gary M. Burge, Series Editor
Wheaton, Illinois

FINDING THE LOST IMAGES OF GOD

PREFACE

MY INTEREST in the Bible's cultural context goes back to 1978, the year I made my first cross-cultural trip. Our program was dedicated to exposing students to the lands of the Bible. Along with the predictable culture shock I experienced in the Eastern Mediterranean, I also suffered a "theological shock" studying Scripture in the regions where all of its stories took place. As I walked over hills that ancient Israelites walked, as I listened to shepherds calling their sheep, as I touched ancient walls and saw the world of my spiritual forbears, I realized that my former feelings of familiarity with the Bible were the result of many skewed preconceptions. That experience was so transforming that I've returned to Israel numerous times, only to experience more "aftershocks."

Understanding the cultural texture of Scripture—what I call its "contexture"—is critical to good biblical interpretation. Thankfully, the ancient world is available to us in the writings and ruins of antiquity as well as in the societies that have retained a good bit of cultural continuity. From that world we learn about institutions that became metaphors for some of the Bible's central truths.

If you asked ancient Israelites to describe God, they might have answered that God was their rock, shield, or maker—using tangible images from their everyday existence. The preferred images would range from the majestic world of kings to the intimate world of parents. In these pages, I invite you to discover seven ordinary, concrete images through which God framed a relationship with his people. I invite you to see how he also longs to use these images to build a relationship with you and me today. If we allow ourselves some reflection time, they will grip our imagination and permanently shape our view of the God we worship. Grounded more in the culture of the biblical world, we will gain a more biblical worldview.

As I say to travelers on our educational journeys, "Let's get on the bus. There's a *lot* to see!"

Chapter 1

THE DIVINE ARCHITECT AND HIS TEMPLE

❋

URBANIZED CIVILIZATIONS across our world are marked by the presence of monumental architecture. Imagine New York City without the Empire State Building or Paris without the Eiffel Tower. Our children spent their early years in downtown Boston, where, from our rooftop, they learned to identify Fenway Park, the Hancock Tower, and the "Pu" (Prudential Building), one of my oldest son's first words. With its changing colors, the Citgo sign in Kenmore Square was always the most interesting.

In our day mammoth city structures are often monuments to human enterprise and architectural creativity. By contrast, colossal architecture in the distant past stood as a tribute to the kings who designed them and to the gods they believed had inspired them.

Central to the architectural vision in the ancient civilizations of the Fertile Crescent was a sense of unique connection between the human and divine realm. The construction of an urban temple-palace complex began with the identification of a unique intersection between heaven and earth. There would

sit a divinely certified regal-ritual city. Even in remains uninhabited for millennia, you can hear the sounds of sacrificial animals in their temple stalls, smell the delicacies from the marketplace, and see the magnificent royal gardens. Cities were the symbolic center of human life even for those who lived in remote rural areas.

KING GUDEA'S HANDS FOLDED OVER STOMACH AND "BLUEPRINT" OF THE TEMPLE OF THE GOD NINGIRSU. IN THE ANCIENT NEAR EAST, BLUEPRINTS WERE THOUGHT TO COME FROM HEAVENLY REVELATIONS.

FOUNDATION TABLETS FROM NIMRUD. THE LAYING OF FOUNDATION STONES WAS MADE INTO A RITUAL.

Ancient Near Eastern kings designed and built the primary buildings, making them public and sacred, not private and secular. Their blueprints were thought to come from heavenly revelations. Laying foundation stones was a ritual. The culmination of a temple-building project sparked communal joy and invited divine inhabitation. These cultural details color the biblical account of creation and the shrines that God chose to inhabit.

A Design-Built Universe

As the Bible's drama begins, God is at work building a universe. Prior to creation, the earth was formless and empty (Gen. 1:2). The Architect began by organizing both space and time, placing boundaries between light and darkness, between the waters above and below the earth's sky, between the sea and dry land, and between night and day. Then God populated these various domains with plants, lights, and creatures, climaxing with the creation of humans to rule over all the earth (1:26). God was pleased with his "very good" creation, and at its completion he entered a permanent "rest" (1:31; 2:2).

This account of creation may be familiar to us, but have you ever considered it as an account of architecture? As a cosmic building project? Other passages of Scripture abound with images of construction. Look at what the psalmist wrote about the Lord's act of primordial creation:

The Creation, from the Luther Bible. c.1530, German School, (16th century)/Bible Society, London, UK /The Bridgeman Art Library

THE CREATION, FROM THE LUTHER BIBLE C. 1530. THE BIBLICAL CREATION STORY SHOULD BE READ AS AN ACCOUNT OF COSMIC ARCHITECTURAL ACTIVITY.

> The LORD wraps himself in light as with a garment;
>> he stretches out the heavens like a tent
>> and lays the beams of his upper chambers on their waters.
> He makes the clouds his chariot
>> and rides on the wings of the wind
> He makes winds his messengers,
>> flames of fire his servants.
> He set the earth on its foundations;
>> it can never be moved.
> You covered it with the watery depths as with a garment;
>> the waters stood above the mountains. . . .
> You set a boundary they cannot cross;
>> never again will they cover the earth. (Ps. 104:2 – 9, emphasis added)

God declared, "My own hand laid the foundations of the earth, and my right hand spread out the heavens; when I summon them, they all stand up together" (Isa. 48:13).

The divine Architect challenged Job's finite knowledge by peppering him with rhetorical questions:

> Where were you when I laid the earth's foundation?
>> Tell me, if you understand.
> Who marked off its dimensions? Surely you know!
>> Who stretched a measuring line across it?
> On what were its footings set,
>> or who laid its cornerstone —
> while the morning stars sang together
>> and all the angels shouted for joy?
>
> Who shut up the sea behind doors
>> when it burst forth from the womb. . .
> when I fixed limits for it
>> and set its doors and bars in place. (Job 38:4 – 10)

Nestled in these references to construction — marking, measuring lines, footings, cornerstone, doors, and bars — is a striking image of singing stars and joyful angels. God's cosmic creation was accompanied by a delighted chorus of heavenly hosts. Wisdom, pictured as a person, recounts this exuberance in Proverbs 8:

I was there when he set the heavens in place,
    when he marked out the horizon on the face of the deep,
when he established the clouds above
    and fixed securely the fountains of the deep,
when he gave the sea its boundary
    so the waters would not overstep his command,
and when he marked out the foundations of the earth.
    Then I was the craftsman at his side.
I was filled with delight day after day,
    rejoicing always in his presence,
rejoicing in his whole world
    and delighting in mankind. *(Prov. 8:27–31, emphasis added)*

These passages amplify the Genesis account of creation and explain God's positive assessment of his work and his following repose. The wise Architect with well-crafted plans deliberately executed the creation of the world without help. His creativity stunned a celestial crowd of spectators. The "show" continues too for those of us who stop in wonder.

I once led a mission team of Malaysians into the jungles of northern Thailand to construct a mission building. My experience as a carpenter made me a likely choice, but my knowledge of building was limited to my own experience in the United States. We built with 2x4s and 2x6s made of teak! The tribal villagers, whose own homes were made of bamboo and straw, lined up along the newly framed floor, looking on with amazement. Like the angels, they were spectators, expressing their awe as they watched a colossal building project. A building whose plans came from afar. A building that would endure, in their minds, forever.

THE EARTH AS GOD'S TEMPLE

Ancient royal texts reveal that the first chapter of Genesis is not only a building story; it is a *temple*-building story. The Sumerian ruler Gudea recorded a detailed account of a temple he built in the ancient city of Lagash, showing homage to its patron god Ningirsu. In response to a divine building plan, Gudea enthusiastically set out to collect wood and precious

FOUNDATION TABLET FROM THE TEMPLE OF NINGIRSU, BUILT BY GUDEA.

stones, and to build it in the proper place. "It being the right field, he laid the measuring cords [on it], drove in stakes at its borders, and checked [the measurements] himself. It was cause for rejoicing for him."[1] The gods then settled into the sanctuary, and Gudea and his people feasted for seven days.

Gudea's temple-building account is typical among ancient Near Eastern compositions. These texts speak of commissioning, preparation, praise, dedication, and blessing. In the Scripture references we have surveyed, we can draw an intriguing parallel between Gudea's work and God's activity of building; each portrays direct, personal involvement and pleasure.

The idea that God built our world as a temple for himself is reinforced through some fascinating and unmistakable correspondences between the construction of a physical tabernacle and God's creation of the world. The tabernacle instructions in Exodus 25 – 31 and the construction descriptions in chapters 35 – 40 are laced with allusions to the first two chapters of Genesis. Moses was fully aware that the tabernacle was meant to be a carefully designed and sanctioned microcosm of the world God built and inhabits. It was a second divinely conceived building project, reminding worshipers that the whole world is God's sanctuary.

RECONSTRUCTION OF THE TABERNACLE

Corresponding to the seven days of creation, God delivered seven speeches to Moses about his design of the sacred tent in Exodus 25–31. Like Genesis 1, the tabernacle instructions begin with a revelation of God's presence and end with a reference to the Sabbath (Ex. 19; 31:12–18). Sabbath in Genesis represents the culmination of seven days during which God speaks his preordered world into existence. The phrase "God

RECONSTRUCTION OF THE BRONZE LAVER

RECONSTRUCTION OF THE ARK OF THE COVENANT

had finished the work" in Genesis 2:2 is echoed in Exodus 40:33: "so Moses finished the work."

Several more subtle correlations link creation and tabernacle accounts. The special term for celestial light sources (ʿōr), used five times in Genesis 1:14–16, is redeployed six times in Exodus with reference to the oil-lit lamps.[2] The waters and the sea provide another obvious connection. "Water" is mentioned eight times in Genesis 1 and "sea" four times; "water" reappears in the bronze laver of water in Exodus 30:18, later to be called "the Sea" in Solomon's temple (1 Kings 7:23). The gold and onyx in Genesis 2:11–12 is also present in the priestly garments in Exodus 25:3–7. The cherubim who guard God's personal sanctuary (Gen. 3) become the guardians of his sacred presence atop the ark of the covenant (Ex. 25:18–22).

On the sixth day of creation, God formed humans and commissioned them to rule the earth—partially defined in Genesis 2:15 as, literally, to "work" and "guard" the garden. Later these two terms are paired to describe the work of priests (Num. 3:7–8). Like the creation of human beings on the sixth day, it is precisely in the sixth section of Exodus 25–31 that the work of the tabernacle craftsmen is described (31:1–11). Leading this group was Bezalel (Ex. 31:2; 36:1–2), a man endowed with the same "Spirit of God" that supervised the creation of the world and gave divine breath to Adam (Gen. 1:2; 2:7).

In the descriptions of the tabernacle construction, its name *miškān* is repeated fifteen times in Exodus 25 – 31 and twenty-eight times in chapters 36 – 40. This word is built on the Hebrew root *šākan*, "to dwell," and refers to God's semi-nomadic dwelling place. The term "tent (of meeting)" is used thirty times in these two sections of Exodus, reinforcing the idea of the tabernacle as God's tent. God's intent *to build* is fused with his intent *to inhabit*. (We'll discuss more implications of living in God's household in chapter 7.)

God's earthly sanctuaries reflected both a heavenly and an earthly pattern. *The temple furnished a unique glimpse of heaven on earth, while simultaneously reminding worshipers that God's temple was earth itself* (see Ps. 78:69). At the consecration of his shrine, Solomon rightly wondered, "But will God really dwell on earth? The heavens, even the highest heaven, cannot contain you. How much less this temple I have built!" (1 Kings 8:27; see Isa. 66:1).

THE HEAVENLY TEMPLE

The God who carefully constructed the world laid a plan before Moses for the building of a tabernacle—a heavenly plan that was also reflected in the temple built by Solomon and rebuilt by his successors (Ex. 25:9, 40; 1 Chron. 28:12, 19). The writer of Hebrews describes Jesus' priestly ministry as superior to humans who minister in

The dedication of the temple, Hole, William Brassey (1846-1917)/Private Collection/© Look and Learn/The Bridgeman Art Library

TEMPLE BEING FILLED WITH THE "SMOKE FROM THE GLORY OF GOD"

CLOUD GUIDING ISRAEL THROUGH THE DESERT

these shrines because they served in sanctuaries that only copied and shadowed the tabernacle of heaven. "This is why Moses was warned when he was about to build the tabernacle: 'See to it that you make everything according to the pattern shown you on the mountain'" (Heb. 8:5). As the true high priest, Jesus entered the heavenly Most Holy Place in the "greater and more perfect tabernacle that is not made with human hands" (Heb. 9:11). The descriptions of a heavenly temple in the book of Hebrews suggest that Moses was given more than a blueprint *from* heaven. He was given a vision *of* heaven.

The book of Revelation offers more visions of the kind of temple that heaven represents. Those who survive the tribulation will "serve [God] day and night in his temple; and he who sits on the throne will shelter them with his presence [lit., spread his tent over them]" (Rev. 7:15). Tabernacle and temple imagery are deliberately mixed. In Revelation 11:1 John is given a rod to measure the temple. You might expect a record of measurements like those in Ezekiel, but none follow. First we catch a glimpse of the temple and the ark of the covenant (11:19). In 15:8 this heavenly temple is filled with "smoke from the glory of God." This same cloud guided Israel through the desert and filled the tabernacle and temple on earth.[3]

The most startling temple reference is in the final section of Revelation. A new heaven and new earth come into view, and a new Jerusalem descends from heaven (Rev. 21). The city is bejeweled and fortified with high walls and twelve pearl gates, and it is supported by twelve decorated foundations. Then an angel with a measuring rod announces the city's dimensions. Like Ezekiel's temple, the new Jerusalem is a cube. John's revelation nears its end with a discovery: *"I did not see a temple in the city, because the Lord God Almighty and the Lamb are its temple. The city does not need the sun or the moon to shine on it, for the glory of God gives it light, and the Lamb is its lamp"* (Rev. 21:22–23, emphasis added).

All of heaven is a temple because God inhabits it.

GOD'S TEMPLE ON EARTH

At the time of Jesus, Jewish life centered around the temple. Commerce, education, religion, and politics all found their hub in the halls and porticos ringing the magnificent shrine built by King Herod. When Jesus entered the temple, he saw it, with prophetic eyes, as a place misused for personal and political gain. Angered, Jesus challenged its corrupt leaders: "Destroy

The New Jerusalem, number 80 from 'The Apocalypse of Angers', 1373–87, Bataille, Nicolas (fl. 1363–1400)/ Musée des Tapisseries, Angers, France/Giraudon/The Bridgeman Art Library

REPRESENTATION OF THE NEW JERUSALEM.

HEROD'S MAGNIFICENT TEMPLE

this temple, and I will raise it again in three days" (John 2:19). In bewilderment they reminded him that the impressive temple had taken forty-six years to rebuild. Jesus, a builder by trade, needed no reminders about the time it took to build such an edifice. They were simply blind to his meaning that the temple he would resurrect would be his body (John 2:21; see Mark 14:58).

This explanation contains a reminder that God's presence—more than any architectural features of a building—defines the temple. As only Jesus could know, the imposing structure before them would fall within a generation. You can see

THE IMPRESSIVE STONE WALLS OF HEROD'S TEMPLE.

FINDING THE LOST IMAGES OF GOD

the uncovered rubble of its walls today. In contrast, the temple of Christ's body would last forever. A literal translation of John 1:14 reads, "The Word became flesh and *tabernacled* among us, and we beheld his *glory*" (emphasis added). The same glory that inhabited the ancient temple was before their eyes in human form.

The notion of a virtual, living temple is important to Paul's theology about the church—the body of Christ (1 Cor. 12)—and his own role in "building" it.

> *For we are co-workers in God's service; you are God's field, God's building.*
>
> *By the grace God has given me, I laid a foundation as a wise builder, and someone else is building on it. But each one should build with care. For no one can lay any foundation other than the one already laid, which is Jesus Christ. If anyone builds on this foundation using gold, silver, costly stones, wood, hay or straw, their work will be shown for what it is, because the Day will bring it to light. It will be revealed with fire, and the fire will test the quality of each person's work.* (1 Cor. 3:9 – 13)

Paul reserved for himself the role of expert builder or architect in contrast to pretenders, but his focus was ultimately on the nature of the foundation, Christ. People in

RUBBLE OF THE TEMPLE STILL REMAINS FROM ITS DESTRUCTION IN AD 70.

© 1995 Phoenix Data Systems

BUILDINGS OF CORINTH WERE
MADE OF SLABS OF MARBLE.

Roman cities were in constant fear of fire with so many buildings, closely built or connected and poorly constructed. Therefore Paul's words would have captured a central image of daily life for his readers, adding strength to his statement that any attempt to erect a cheap and fragile building out of wood, hay, or straw would only lead to its destruction in the fire of judgment. Worse, such buildings would constitute an insult to a foundation designed to support a magnificent superstructure. The church, in Paul's mind, is meant to assume its position on this stable foundation like slabs of marble brought from Laconia into Corinth for public buildings or like the mammoth stones used in the temple at Jerusalem (1 Chron. 29:2).

Paul continued with an explicit statement about what this building is: "Don't you know that you yourselves are God's temple and that God's Spirit dwells in your midst? If anyone destroys God's temple, God will destroy that person; for God's temple is sacred, and you together are that temple" (1 Cor. 3:16–17). Like Jesus, Paul mentioned a destruction of the temple, a dreaded reoccurrence in Israel's history. But Paul was referring to the virtual temple of Christ's body, which is at risk from more subtle forms of pollution and destruction.

Cornerstone and Capstone

The image of God's people as a temple resurfaces in Ephesians 2, this time with the apostles and prophets as the foundation and "Christ Jesus himself as the chief cornerstone. In him the whole building is joined together and rises to become a holy temple in the Lord. And in him you too are being built together to become a dwelling in which God lives by his Spirit" (Eph. 2:20–22). This passage enlists a prophetic verse: "See, I lay a stone in Zion, a tested stone, a precious cornerstone for a sure foundation; the one who relies on it will never be stricken with panic" (Isa. 28:16).

The cornerstones in monumental buildings of the first century were massive stones that anchored the lapped stones above. In Herod's temple the lower foundation stones weighed about 570 tons with a width of fourteen feet and a length of more than fifty feet. The space between the megaton building blocks was often so minute that even today you can barely slide a piece of paper between them! Teams of expert builders would join hewn and smoothed stones, pinning them in place with dowels. Temples that still stand today, two thousand years later, attest to the skilled craftsmanship involved in building properly from the ground up.

Baker Photo Archive

CORNERSTONE OF THE TEMPLE MOUNT.

© 1995 Phoenix Data Systems

CAPSTONE

Some scholars believe that the uncommon and ambiguous word translated "cornerstone" can also refer to a "capstone." It is used in the Bible only here, in 1 Peter 2:6, and in the early Greek version of Isaiah 28:16, to which both New Testament passages allude. The capstone is the final stone that anchors an archway and completes a building. This too is a fitting image of Christ who holds together the whole "building" of believers in Ephesians 2. In support of this we find a subsequent verse in 1 Peter 2:7 that quotes Psalm 118:22: "The stone the builders rejected has become the cornerstone [read: capstone]." Here the phrase refers to the finishing stone which, if on the ground, could cause someone to trip or, worse, kill someone if it fell from above (Luke 20:17–18).

LIVING STONES, BUILT UP

Paul used an unusual verb in Ephesians 2 to illustrate fitting stones together. It reappears in the Ephesians 4, describing the church in organic, physiological terms: "From him the whole body, joined and held together by every supporting ligament, grows and builds itself up in love, as each part does its work" (Eph. 4:16). The apostle's image of a spiritual building (or body) focuses our attention on both a sure foundation and an intimate fellowship. We are "joined together" and "built together" (Eph. 2:21–22).

God's desire to build a living, interconnected temple in which to live gave focus to Paul's ministry. He knew that this outcome required continuous joint effort at "up-building," a term usually translated "edifying." A variety of words from this root are put to use throughout the Corinthian letters to convey the same image in Ephesians. To both churches Paul described the purpose of all spiritual gifts as the *upbuilding* of the body.[4] He also engages the term to defend his ministry's mission — to *build up* believers and not to tear them down (2 Cor. 13:10). Peter had a similar idea: "As you come to him, the living Stone — rejected by humans but chosen by God and precious to him — you also, like living stones, are being built into a spiritual house to be a holy priesthood, offering spiritual sacrifices acceptable to God through Jesus Christ" (1 Peter 2:4 – 5).

FAITH AND THE DIVINE ARCHITECT

As a former carpenter, I still recall the unique sense of accomplishment when a building project comes together. When a foundation of interlocking bricks is complete, sitting level around a cement pad. When a wall of studs and plywood is heaved into place and joined to another one beside it. When precut rafters are nailed to a ridge pole and a triangle of joists ties their bases together. When the building is "buttoned up"

Todd Bolen/www.BiblePlaces.com

SOME OF THE LARGE STONES OF THE TEMPLE ARE SO CLOSE THAT A PIECE OF PAPER CAN BARELY BE SLID BETWEEN THEM!

BUILDERS HAVE A SENSE OF
ACCOMPLISHMENT WHEN THEY SEE A
PROJECT COMING TOGETHER.

with roof shingles and windows. I can barely imagine the feeling of completing a skyscraper.

I *can't* imagine creating the world!

Just as the Empire State Building distinguishes New York, or the Eiffel Tower, Paris, creation and the church are God's signature architectural achievements. Of the two only the church is still under construction. As followers of Christ, the Bible describes us as living stones in a temple inhabited by God's Spirit. Making this leap may require us to stretch our imaginations. But it's worth the effort. Images of the divine Architect open a window into heaven where the angels sing over God's construction project called earth. It gives us room and reason to rejoice when new stones are added to the church, held together by the Chief Cornerstone.

As you consider these stones, carefully chosen and tightly fitted together, remember that we are inextricably connected to each other in community. We are bound together for mutual "upbuilding" and for the worship of this world's Architect. As the writer of Hebrews said, "Every house is built by someone, but God is the builder of everything . . . and *we are his house*" (Heb. 3:4, 6, emphasis added).

Chapter 2

THE DIVINE ARTISAN AND HIS IMAGES

HAVE YOU ever noticed the universal fascination with human craftsmanship? Whether an artisan's medium is stone, wood, gems, fabric, metal, paint, glass, or pottery, we find ourselves suspended in time, mesmerized, watching them at work. Crowds gather at booths in a craft fair. Kids stare out the car windows at a building site where cranes hoist beams into place. Friends find it impossible not to peer at a half-painted canvas in progress.

Something about humans at work calls for our attention.

When I was in Hebron in southern Israel many years ago, I sat for tea with fellow students, watching artisans at work. Across the street from the burial sites of Israel's patriarchs and matriarchs, craftsmen dipped long tubes into white hot liquid glass, then blew and spun the mass into stunning creations. Next door a potter kicked a wheel at his feet, rotating the round table. At first his creation appeared to be a simple, cone-shaped object. Then he pressed his wet hands into the spinning clay, coaxing new dimensions. We could have watched for hours. Each item the potter "brought to life" elicited "ahhs"

A POTTER FORMING THE CLAY.
© Mike Goldwater/Alamy

CRAFTSMAN AT WORK BLOWING GLASS.

from the small crowd of awed spectators. As with the glass-blower's handmade pieces, the potter's every vase, pitcher, and cup were unique.

It turns out that pottery is one of the most helpful remains for studying ancient Israel. In archaeological digs, potsherds (broken pieces of pottery) abound beyond all other artifacts. Everything from simple domestic bowls to expensive com-

MIDDLE EASTERN POTTER WORKING AT THE POTTER'S WHEEL.

Z. Radovan/www.BibleLandPictures.com

VARIOUS FORMS OF ANCIENT POTTERY. POTTERY IS ONE OF THE MOST HELPFUL REMAINS FOR STUDYING ANCIENT ISRAEL.

mercial containers could be made from mud that was molded, dried by the sun or in a kiln, and then plastered or painted. Because it is so common, pottery provides archaeologists with a reliable guide for dating ancient occupation and witnessing the cultural influences that are mapped out on their surfaces.

Sadly, one of those influences is idolatry.

With uncommon poignancy, the Bible pictures God as an artisan at work with

Baker Photo Archive, courtesy of the Eretz Israel Museum

MAN-MADE IDOL CREATED FROM CLAY.

his hands, forming humans out of the earth's dust. Biblical authors relied on the relationship between a craftsman and his handiwork to explain God's sovereign purposes—and the absurdity of human defiance. They also used sarcasm to lampoon the worship of man-made idols. As we land in the New Testament, we discover rich encouragement for God's masterpieces, each destined to be conformed to the "image of Christ."

MAKING HUMANS

After the grand account of the building of the cosmos in Genesis 1, a second, more intimate description of the formation of the first human couple follows in chapter 2. Genesis 1 employs a term for "create" that is reserved exclusively for God. The second chapter introduces a common term used for human potters and other artisans, *yâṣar*, meaning "to form or fashion." "The Lord God *formed* a man from the dust of the ground and breathed into his nostrils the breath of life, and the man became a living being . . . and [in Eden] he put the man he had

THE CREATION OF EVE.

formed" (Gen. 2:7–8, emphasis added). Later psalmists praised the God who "*forms* the hearts of all" (Ps. 33:15, emphasis added) and *fashioned* every day of our lives in advance (Ps. 139:16).

The making of Eve resolved the only aspect of creation God declared "not good"—the need for Adam to have a "helper suitable for him" (Gen. 2:18, 20). "Then the Lord God made a woman from the rib he had taken out of the man, and he brought her to the man" (Gen. 2:22). The choice of Hebrew verbs once again employs the imagery of a craftsman. God literally "built" Eve from the side of Adam.

The first man, ʾādām, was made from the dust of the ground, ʾᵃdāmā, in Genesis 2:7. This word-play in Hebrew reinforces the "earthy" dimension of humans, as does the dust, which comes to symbolize frailty and death. In the curse that followed the couple's disobedience, God said, "For dust you are and to dust you will return" (Gen. 3:19). Thankfully, he treats us tenderly because he "remembers that we are dust"

THE BABYLONIAN CREATION STORY OF THE ATRAHASIS EPIC.

EGYPTIAN GOD MAKING A HUMAN FROM CLAY ON HIS POTTER'S WHEEL.

(Ps. 103:14). Into chosen dust God breathed life. Without this breath no human can live. God's power to bring new life to his people is pictured as a new breath or spirit that he blows into them (Ezek. 37; John 20:22; Acts 2).

Mythical accounts from the ancient Near East echo the biblical understanding of humans as being both earthly and divine. In the Babylonian creation story *Atrahasis*, humans are made from the blood of a slain deity mixed with clay. The Egyptian god Khnum is pictured making humans from clay on his potter's wheel. These stories reveal that ancient communities shared a common notion that God personally and purposefully crafted the first humans out of the ground and shared with them a part of his divinity. In Genesis 1 the words "image" and "likeness" of God imply this unique mix. We'll pick up the topic of divine images in a moment. But let's look first at the ongoing biblical significance of God's "treasure" being in "jars of clay" (2 Cor. 4:7).

CLAY IN THE POTTER'S HANDS

The place is Judah. The time is about 600 BC, the eve of catastrophe. The northern kingdom had already been destroyed by the Assyrians, and Jerusalem would hardly remain invincible before the onrushing Babylonians. In this crisis God instructs Jeremiah to go to a potter's house to receive a prophetic message.

> So I went down to the potter's house, and I saw him working at the wheel. But the pot he was shaping from the clay was marred in his hands; so the potter formed it into another pot, shaping it as seemed best to him.
> Then the word of the LORD came to me. He said, "Can I not do with you, Israel, as this potter does?" declares the LORD. "Like clay in the hand of the potter, so are you in my hand, Israel." (Jer. 18:3–6)

The craftsman's daily routine provided the prophet with an apt parable. Potters used two horizontal stone wheels joined by a shaft, rotating the lower one by foot, and they handled chunks of suitable clay on the spinning top one. As necessary, the potter kneaded the clay, removed foreign objects, added tempering elements, and applied water to keep the clay supple.

RECONSTRUCTION OF ANCIENT POTTER'S WHEEL

After drying and decoration, a pot would be ready for the kiln's 1,500-degree fires.

On this particular day, however, Jeremiah witnessed *God* at work.

Fundamentally, the potter has every right to do with his clay as he wants (Rom. 9:20–21). Flexible and responsive, clay can be reshaped, even after being "marred" (Jer. 18:4). Though the Hebrew word here suggests being spoiled, the potter is resolute to a point. However, once clay has hardened in the wrong shape, it is tossed out as rubbish. (Potters produce a lot of trash!) God was intent on offering nations an opportunity to repent if they responded to his hand. But he was also "preparing [lit., *forming*] a disaster" (18:11) for his own people because their idolatry had contributed to an irretrievable hardening of heart (vv. 7–9, 15).

In the next chapter Jeremiah returned to the potter for a more devastating message from the Lord:

> This is what the LORD says: "Go and buy a clay jar from a potter. Take along some of the elders of the people and of the priests and go out to the Valley of Ben Hinnom, near the entrance of the Potsherd Gate. There proclaim the words I tell you, and say, 'Hear the word of the LORD,

you kings of Judah and people of Jerusalem. . . . Listen! I am going to bring a disaster on this place that will make the ears of everyone who hears of it tingle. For they have forsaken me and made this a place of foreign gods; they have burned incense in it to gods that neither they nor their ancestors nor the kings of Judah ever knew, and they have filled this place with the blood of the innocent.'" (Jer. 19:1–4)

The Hinnom Valley ran along the southwestern edge of Jerusalem, near Temple Mount. The potter's quarter was located here probably because of its proximity to the temple (for which many vessels were made), the available clay and water, and the dump that lay conveniently at hand. Tragically, in this valley—at a place called "Topheth," which literally translates "fire pit"—the people of Judah had been sacrificing their children in fire offerings to the god Baal (Jer. 19:5–6).[5] God had watched too long as his people engaged in the same idolatrous practices that had caused pagans to be expelled from Canaan in the first place.

The divine Potter was about to smash his chosen city and make it like Topheth, giving the people the outcome on which they were bent—their children's annihilation (v. 9). He told Jeremiah to break the jar and announce, "This is what the LORD Almighty says: 'I will smash this nation and this city just as

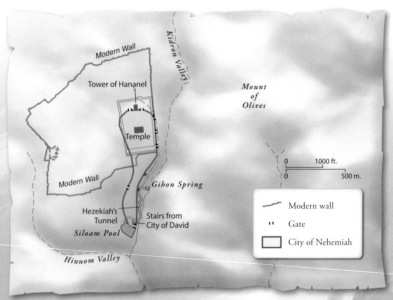

OLD TESTAMENT JERUSALEM. THE HINNOM VALLEY RUNS ALONG THE SOUTHERN SIDE OF THE TEMPLE MOUNT.

this potter's jar is smashed and cannot be repaired. They will bury the dead in Topheth until there is no more room.... I will make this city like Topheth'" (Jer. 19:11–12).

The symbolic breaking of a pot was used in the Near East like a voodoo doll, as a magical way to prompt the suffering of one's enemies. Egyptians ceremonially destroyed statuettes or pottery vessels with the names of state enemies and curses inscribed on them. The shattering of pots became a common description of a city's annihilation. In Jeremiah, we find God preparing destruction *for his own people*. He vowed to break his own "pottery" because their hearts, like clay, were "hardened" (Jer. 19:15; NIV trans. the Heb. word "stiff-necked"). "It's no use," the people admitted. They challenged the Lord with the absurdity of clay challenging its potter: "We will continue with our own plans; we will all follow the stubbornness of our evil hearts" (18:12).

IDOLS AND IMAGES

Israel's faith in man-made idols instead of its Creator constitutes one of the central examples of religious irony in the book of Jeremiah. The Hinnom Valley was one of many places where people worshiped foreign gods. In Jeremiah 10 the prophet conveys God's disgust with a people who (should) know their real Creator.

> *For the practices of the peoples are worthless;*
> > *they cut a tree out of the forest,*
> > *and a craftsman shapes it with his chisel.*
> *They adorn it with silver and gold;*
> > *they fasten it with hammer and nails*
> > *so it will not totter.*
> *Like a scarecrow in a cucumber field,*
> > *their idols cannot speak;*
> *they must be carried*
> > *because they cannot walk.*
> *Do not fear them;*
> > *they can do no harm*
> > *nor can they do any good. (Jer. 10:3–5).*

God's people are afraid of what is nothing but wood and metal. These idols are a burden, Jeremiah says sarcastically, for they can neither walk nor talk. Yet they are made from the finest silver and gold. What is more, craftsmen dress them in blue and purple, a color denoting royalty (v. 9). In the face of this travesty the prophet responds, "*But the L*ORD *is the true God; he is the living God, the eternal King*" (v. 10, emphasis added).

Jeremiah is not alone in his parody of "god-making." Isaiah offers numerous caricatures of idolatry. Isaiah pokes at humans who worship a god they have to nail down to keep from toppling (Isa. 41:7). Repeating the artisan term "form" in chapter 44, Isaiah contrasts these human craftsmen with the God who creates and rules the universe. Manufacturing idols was big business in Isaiah's world. The smiths and carpenters were skilled at plating images with metal and decorating them with ornaments. But they were men who grew fatigued in their work (44:12). To warm themselves, they burned leftover wood from the logs they were carving (v. 16). From these everyday materials they created figurines "in human form, human form *in all its glory*,[6] that it may dwell in a shrine" (v. 13, emphasis added). There these lifeless, speechless, and powerless idols were entreated, "Save me! You are my god!" (v. 17).

The irony is unmistakable. The sarcasm is scathing.

When you read texts from the ancient Near East, it's clear that idolatry had more theological sophistication than is suggested in these prophetic parodies. Yes, there was elaborate craftsmanship. In many temples the impotent idols were washed, dressed, and fed daily. Yet the practice of worshiping wood or metal was refined by the belief

JEREMIAH SAYS THAT MAN-MADE IDOLS ARE WORTHLESS, AND YET MADE OF FINE METALS SUCH AS SILVER AND GOLD.

FINDING THE LOST IMAGES OF GOD

that a spirit animated the idols only during a special ceremony of inspiration. This ceremony is called in some texts *mis pi*, or "the opening of the mouth." In a typical scenario, carvers would go to a sacred grove along a river and build the idol to ritual specifications. Then, prior to dawn, the craftsman placed the idol in a boat and sent it to the other shore. Ritual participants awaited the idol's spirit inhabitation at about the point it reached mid-river. Once inhabited, the idol was enshrined.

While the prophets had no patience for the subtleties of pagan ideology, their rituals bring nuance to the Genesis 2 account. The picture of a divine being breathing into an "image" made out of soil sounds much like the process of idol-making. This is especially true when you consider that God explicitly made humans in his own likeness and image, just as humans do with their idols. God placed Adam and Eve in his garden sanctuary in a way that resembles the placement of an idol in a temple. These parallels suggest one of many reasons why Israel was forbidden to make images of any kind. Images of humans in particular were odious because *God had already made humans as an image of himself!* The world was meant to have access to God's "icons" by looking to real human beings who care for this world on his behalf.[7] Our "glory" (Ps. 8:5) is derived from the God whose likeness we share.

It is utterly backward to make *God* in *our* image.

Human Image-Bearers

The notion that God crafted humans as his image-bearers carries enormous implications, some of which we'll explore in the chapter on the divine Monarch and his regents. For now we want to drink deeply from the idea that God formed humans individually, with intentionality and value. This understanding couldn't be more beautifully expressed than in the poetic sentiments of Psalm 139:

> *For you created my inmost being;*
> *   you knit me together in my mother's womb.*
> *I praise you because I am fearfully and wonderfully made;*
> *   your works are wonderful,*
> *   I know that full well.*

> *My frame was not hidden from you*
>> *when I was made in the secret place,*
>> *when I was woven together in the depths of the earth.*
> *Your eyes saw my unformed body;*
>> *all the days ordained for me were written in your book*
>> *before one of them came to be.*
> *How precious to me are your thoughts, God!*
>> *How vast is the sum of them!* (Ps. 139:13 – 17)

Although God banished the first couple from paradise, he did not do so without continuing to care for them. Nor did they cease their role as his image-bearers. When Noah and his family emerged from the ark to repopulate the earth, God declared manslaughter a capital crime on this basis: "Whoever sheds human blood, by humans shall their blood be shed; *for in the image of God has God made mankind*" (Gen. 9:6, emphasis added). A fundamental biblical ethic is articulated here. God has a stake in how humans are treated because they carry his image and likeness. The same principle is at work in the proverb, "Whoever oppresses the poor shows contempt for their Maker, but whoever is kind to the needy honors God" (Prov. 14:31).

The ethical dimension of image-bearing comes up subtly in one of Jesus' confrontations with leaders who tried to trap him. The question was whether Jews should pay taxes to Rome. Jesus asked whose image (Gk., *eikōn*) was on the coin. The critics answered, "Caesar's." Then "give back to Caesar what is Caesar's, and to God what is God's," Jesus replied (Matt. 22:21). Jesus characteristically turned a trap that the leaders had set for him into an indictment of themselves. Coins bear the image of the governments that manufacture them; therefore, they may take them back in the form of taxes. But the more important issue is what we do with ourselves as humans, stamped as we are with the divine image. Have we given ourselves fully to God as he deserves? How do we treat others who are also stamped with his likeness?

On occasion, I ask Pastor Mack, a seasoned inner-city pastor, to describe the nature of ministry to the poor and homeless for seminary students in our Urban Ministry Program.

He says, "I try to look deep down inside to find the image of God, and then I try to help them to see it." That speaks volumes, doesn't it?

A DENARIUS PROVIDED A LESSON ON THE IMPLICATIONS OF IMAGE-BEARING.

Paul's ethics take the image of God even further. According to the apostle, Christ came as a second Adam. What Adam had ruined through his trespass, Jesus restored through his gift of righteousness (Rom. 5:12–21). "The first man, Adam, became a living being; the last Adam, a life-giving spirit" (1 Cor. 15:45). To press the analogy further, Jesus is the true "image of the invisible God, the firstborn over all creation" (Col. 1:15). It is to the likeness or image of God's Son that we are "predestined to be conformed" (Rom. 8:29). In language resonating with artisan imagery, Paul writes, "We are God's handiwork, created in Christ Jesus to do good works, which God prepared in advance for us to do" (Eph. 2:10).

Ethics is responding to the hand of the Potter who made us and shapes us for his purposes.

Conformity to the image of Christ leads inevitably to respect, equality, and unity with others who share that identity. "Do not lie to each other, since you have taken off your old self with its practices and have put on the new self, which is being renewed in knowledge *in the image of its Creator*. Here there is no Gentile or Jew, circumcised or uncircumcised, barbarian, Scythian, slave or free, but Christ is all, and is in all" (Col. 3:9–11).

Paul said our true identity is a "new creation" (2 Cor. 5:17). The Artisan of Genesis 2 continues his purposeful and creative work in countless hearts every day. It's up to us to recognize this reality and respond to it.

FAITH AND THE DIVINE ARTISAN

The nineteenth-century sociologist Emile Durkheim summarized religion as humans "making god(s) in our own image." Societies, he believed, take their most important values and ideals and convert them into celestial deities and myths. While the Bible offers us revelation of a God who makes us in his own image, it shares Durkheim's assessment of how religion degenerates into the opposite. In our day, we have crafted gods of individualism, consumerism, security, prosperity, and health. We nurture a god who is love without justice and blessing without commitment, who responds to our promise-claiming demands as if he were a god we could manipulate.

Like Jeremiah, Paul warned that people who reverse the image-making order, mistaking creation for the Creator, will be given over eventually to their desires (Rom. 1:20–26). When we give up worshiping God's glory, we end up losing our own glory as his image-bearers. We become what we worship — nothing more than the dust from which we are made.

A trip back to the potter's shop will remind us who is the Potter and who is the clay. How much better to respond to his hands than to challenge his plans!

Chapter 3

THE DIVINE FARMER AND HIS PLANTINGS

OUR WORLD has become urban, mobile, and technologically sophisticated—with interstate commuters on daily jets and international business accomplished with a click. In my own travels I always make sure to have a charged laptop, cables for my iPhone, electrical converters, a GPS, and a couple of hardbound books with a notepad for times without electricity or when the flight attendants tell us to power down our devices. My worst nightmare is the "blue screen of death"—a computer crash—without a backup.

Our lifestyle lacks any discernible ties with our crop-planting ancestors, whose experience was more connected to agricultural space than cyberspace. Their world exists in family stories handed down for some, but for most of us it is accessible only through Hollywood's romanticized re-creations. Our sense of identity is no longer tied to geography, and most of us do not share with those on the other side of field or fence the fear of devastating drought or the joy of harvest.

The Israelites, however, clustered in small villages, where farming meant more than subsistence; it meant life beating

FRUITFUL AND LIVELY VINEYARD.

to an organic rhythm and a worldview grounded in seasonal realities.

Farms, gardens, orchards, and vineyards were, in the best of times, verdant places of fruitfulness, settings that represented livelihood and well-being. A blessed Israel was an Israel in which every man sat under his own vine and fig tree (1 Kings 4:25). By contrast, debilitated and desolate farms represented

DROUGHT AND FAMINE WERE A SIGN OF GOD'S CURSE.

God's curse. Dread of drought and famine — its ravaging sister — were never absent. A good season — with the right amount and timing of fall, winter, and spring rain — could never be taken for granted. It occurred on average about two-thirds of the time.

The Garden Sanctuaries of God

The imagery of a divine Farmer begins long before God's people entered the Promised Land. Genesis 2 provides an intimate portrait of a God who, having structured the universe, turned his attention to a perpetually watered garden and to the humans who could tend it. "The Lord God formed a man from the dust of the ground and breathed into his nostrils the breath of life. . . . Now the Lord God had planted a garden in the east, in Eden; and there he put the man he had formed" (Gen. 2:7–8).

The story of creation reveals a God interested in the senses. In 2:9 God declared all the plants "pleasing to the eye and good for food." Two trees grew in the garden, the first of which, by eating its fruit, served as a source of perpetual vigor and immortality: the Tree of Life. A primal river in the garden refreshed the plants and carried life-nourishing water to distant lands through its four branches.

The garden of Eden was a place of God's dwelling, an exotic sanctuary where the

THE TREE OF LIFE SERVED AS A SOURCE FOR PERPETUAL VIGOR AND IMMORTALITY.

SOLOMON'S TEMPLE WITH ITS INTRICATELY ENGRAVED WALLS.

Lord God walked daily with his human gardeners. Imagine working fertile soil alongside perpetually bubbling streams, breathing in the smell of budding blossoms and sitting down to a feast of fruits and vegetables in every color — an endless buffet of life-sustaining bounty at the invitation of your divine host. That was Eden. There, in their naked innocence, the first couple could enjoy their Maker and each other in continuous, shame-free fellowship. This archetypal garden was marked by both fruitfulness and intimacy. God's command for Adam and Eve to reproduce (Gen. 1:28) was a natural result of that intimacy.

But a second tree grew in the garden — and Adam and Eve's choice to eat its fruit destroyed this sacred intimacy.

Toil and sweat and a rift between man and woman swept into this paradise. Although God barred humans from the garden, its imagery and that of the Gardener would linger throughout Israel's history. Cherubim in Israel's sacred shrine (the temple) guarded the divine presence; a menorah burned day and night, possibly representing the tree of life; and precious stones, and plants, both natural and engraved, adorned its walls[8] (1 Kings 6:29). Eden was God's classic sanctuary, one replicated in Israel's temples, but ultimately "fulfilled" in the heavenly temple of Revelation with its primal river and perpetually nourishing tree of life (Rev. 22:1–2).

POMEGRANATES WERE AND STILL ARE A COMMON CROP IN THE MIDDLE EAST.

A GARDEN FOR LOVERS

Images from Eden reverberate in the Song of Songs. The floral kaleidoscope surrounding the lovers includes the most sense-stimulating and costly items from Africa to China. The woman is herself a fertile paradise.

> *You are a garden locked up, my sister, my bride;*
> *   you are a spring enclosed, a sealed fountain.*
> *Your plants are an orchard of pomegranates*
> *   with choice fruits,*
> *   with henna and nard,*
> *   nard and saffron,*
> *   calamus and cinnamon,*
> *   with every kind of incense tree,*
> *   with myrrh and aloes*
> *   and all the finest spices.*
> *You are a garden fountain,*
> *   a well of flowing water*
> *   streaming down from Lebanon. (Song 4:12 – 15)*

These lyrics—both exotic and erotic—transport us to an idyllic garden resplendent with sights and scents of twenty-four different kinds of plants giving mating clues to the amorous human hind and hart. The lovers, called gazelles, return

GAZELLES, WHICH REPRESENTED TWO LOVERS
IN THE BOOK OF SONG OF SONGS.

in late spring to the apple tree where they were born to consummate their intimacy (Song 8:5). The time of their love is determined by the seasonal cycles to which all nature bends.

> Come, my beloved, let us go to the countryside,
>   let us spend the night in the villages.
> Let us go early to the vineyards
>   to see if the vines have budded,
> if their blossoms have opened,
>   and if the pomegranates are in bloom—
>   there I will give you my love.
> The mandrakes send out their fragrance,
>   and at our door is every delicacy,
> both new and old,
>   that I have stored up for you, my beloved. (Song 7:11–13)

Here in the Bible's vivid poetry we find a sanctified celebration of garden intimacy, a hint of Eden's continued call.

A COVENANT FARM

With the divine Gardener at work in the beginning of human history, farming served as a powerful metaphor through which

God communicated his relationship to his people. As images of Eden shadowed Israel's tabernacle and temple, the Promised Land also recalled God's sacred garden.

Egypt was a lush landscape, watered annually by the Nile. The Israelites' journey away from Egypt's predictable fertility into the arid wilderness showcased God's power and mercy. He turned bitter water sweet, delivered manna every morning, and guided them personally through a cloud and pillar. They would have the privilege of God's bounty on a fruitful farm in Canaan waiting for them — "wells you did not dig, and vineyards and olive groves you did not plant" (Deut. 6:11) — if they served him alone. As he had in Eden, the divine Gardener would provision this special farm with just the right amount of water.

But like Adam, God's tenants would have to be faithful in order to enjoy these benefits. This special land of mountains and valleys "drinks rain from heaven," providing "grass in the fields for . . . cattle" and "grain, new wine and olive oil" for God's people. "You will eat and be satisfied," God promised — if no other gods receive your faith and worship (Deut. 11:11 – 17).

The generation of Israelites that left Egypt did not have the faith to move onto God's farm immediately, even though spies confirmed the land's bounty with a branch of grape clusters, pomegranates, and figs — taken from a valley called Eschol, meaning "cluster."

THE LUSH LANDSCAPE SURROUNDING THE NILE RIVER.

VINES REPRESENT THE PEOPLE OF ISRAEL IN THE PROMISED
LAND. THROUGHOUT THEIR HISTORY THEY WERE PLANTED,
PRUNED, AND EVENTUALLY UPROOTED.

Those without faith in God's promises suffered and died in
the wilderness. The next generation, under the leadership of
Joshua, one of the believing spies, moved in and possessed the
Land of Promise.

By divine decree, the land was first divided into tribal
allotments. God predetermined the tenants for each area of his
farm, underscoring his ultimate ownership in their laws (see
1 Kings 21). Not only would land transfers be reversed during
sabbatical years and the Jubilee, but Israel was never granted
an inalienable right to stay on the farm should they transgress
the covenant. God would shut off the rains as an early warning
sign that their split loyalties to other sources of fertility, such
as Baal, would eventually lead to their eviction. Historically we
know this as "the exile".

GOD'S VINEYARD

Along with these implicit references to Canaan as God's farm
are images of Israel as a vine being planted on that farm. Psalm
80 summarizes the history that led to their "planting" and
eventual uprooting.

> *You transplanted a vine from Egypt;*
> *you drove out the nations and planted it.*
> *You cleared the ground for it,*
> *and it took root and filled the land.*
> *The mountains were covered with its shade,*
> *the mighty cedars with its branches.*
> *Its branches reached as far as the Sea,*
> *its shoots as far as the River.*
> *Why have you broken down its walls*
> *so that all who pass by pick its grapes?*
> *Boars from the forest ravage it,*
> *and insects from the fields feed on it.* (Ps. 80:8 – 13)

The prophets had warned Israel that the divine Farmer had limits on his patience. He was not going to put his energy and resources into a vineyard that failed to produce (see Jer. 2:21). Isaiah, in particular, wielded this image for judicial indictment.

Isaiah penned two songs about vineyards, the first of which carried a stinging rebuke of Israel's fruitlessness. Here you'll find the most fascinating and detailed description of vineyards in the Bible. Though framed as a joyous harvest song, its explanation is ominous.

> *I will sing for the one I love*
> *a song about his vineyard:*
> *My loved one had a vineyard*
> *on a fertile hillside.*
> *He dug it up and cleared it of stones*
> *and planted it with the choicest vines.*
> *He built a watchtower in it*
> *and cut out a winepress as well.*
> *Then he looked for a crop of good grapes,*
> *but it yielded only bad fruit.*
> *"Now you dwellers in Jerusalem and people of Judah,*
> *judge between me and my vineyard.*
> *What more could have been done for my vineyard*
> *than I have done for it?*
> *When I looked for good grapes,*
> *why did it yield only bad?*

BECAUSE OF THE HILLY TERRAIN, VINEYARDS ARE TYPICALLY TERRACED ON HILLSIDES.

> Now I will tell you
>   what I am going to do to my vineyard:
> I will take away its hedge,
>   and it will be destroyed;
> I will break down its wall,
>   and it will be trampled.
> I will make it a wasteland,
>   neither pruned nor cultivated,
>   and briers and thorns will grow there.
> I will command the clouds
>   not to rain on it."
> The vineyard of the LORD Almighty
>   is the nation of Israel,
> and the people of Judah
>   are the vines he delighted in.
> And he looked for justice, but saw bloodshed;
>   for righteousness, but heard cries of distress. (Isa. 5:1–7)

As a harvest song for "my loved one," this parable would have tugged at the sentiments an agrarian people felt during their favorite time of year. Women danced and sang in their vineyards (Judg. 21:21), and, as we have seen, vineyards and gardens were often associated with intimacy. This may even be a wedding song not unlike the Song of Songs in its setting.[9] The prophet begins a judicial indictment by engaging his listeners in a disarming and sentimental way.

The parable follows the familiar though uncommon progression of starting a vineyard "from scratch." This task is like the first work of God, who, it turns out, is the story's real farmer. Establishing a vineyard required a family's investment of backbreaking work over several years. Instead, most families combined their energies simply to *maintain* a terraced farm. Yet the parable's beloved sets out to transform a barren limestone hillside into a fertile vineyard.

To trap rainwater, a farmer must form terraces on the rocky slopes—a chore that exacts hundreds of hours. Visitors to Israel are typically astonished at how many stones are … *everywhere*. Farmers use these rocks to build the walls that separate each terrace and support the soil transferred to them. No level is ever completely free of stones, which provide extra shade and more surface area for dew to collect. The farmer who plants a choice vine will tend it for three to five years before his first grapes are edible. In anticipation of a valuable harvest, the farmer uses the stones to build a watchtower and then cuts limestone from the hillside to form a winepress. He would have continued plowing the terraces to keep away weeds that might

A FARMER WOULD WATCH OVER HIS VINEYARD BY CLIMBING INTO THE WATCHTOWER FOR A BETTER VIEW.

A WINEPRESS ON WHICH THE GRAPES WOULD BE PRESSED AND THE JUICE WOULD FLOW INTO THE LOWER GATHERING CONTAINER.

compete for precious moisture. A "hedge" of thistles would be planted on top of the wall (cf. v. 5) to deter predators.

All of this detail paints a picture of a careful, competent, calculated, and committed farmer who has done everything possible to ensure success. His long-term investment should provide generations with the blessings of grapes, raisins, syrups, and wine. The threefold repetition of the word "wait" (vv. 2, 4, 7 [NIV "looked for"]) captures the feeling of eager and legitimate anticipation. Yet instead of good grapes, the vine produces, literally, "stinking" or "wild" fruit—something agriculturally unimaginable. "What more could I have done?" he asks those who understand his bewilderment (v. 4). He vows to complete a comprehensive reversal of his work: he will tear down the hedge and wall, leave the vine unattended, let briers and thorns grow and "command the clouds not to rain" (vv. 5–6). The prophetic parable certainly now has captured everyone's attention.

At this point it is clear that the song is neither happy nor harmless and that the farmer is no mere human. The prophet explains that this vineyard *of the Lord Almighty* is the house of Israel and the men of Judah are "his pleasant planting" (v. 7 NRSV).[10] Employing a play on words, he mirrors the realities on the farm with realities in the community: He looked for justice (*mišpāṭ*) but saw bloodshed (*miśpāḥ*), for righteousness (*ṣᵉdāqâ*) but heard cries of distress (*ṣᵉᶜāqâ*). What looked like good grapes was, on closer inspection, just the opposite.

Judah tottered on the verge of an inconceivable tragedy. The Assyrians were already on the march. God's people were about to forfeit the farm.

Thankfully, in his second vineyard parable, Isaiah provided a word of hope for the trampled vineyard: "In days to come Jacob will take root, Israel will bud and blossom and fill all the world with fruit" (Isa. 27:6).

THE TRUE VINE

In the intimate company of his disciples on the eve of his death, Jesus recalls this Old Testament imagery and breathes into it new meaning.

"I am the true vine, and my Father is the gardener. He cuts off every branch in me that bears no fruit, while every branch that does bear fruit he prunes so that it will be even more fruitful. You are already clean because of the word I have spoken to you. Remain in me, as I also remain in you. No branch can bear fruit by itself; it

Todd Bolen/www.BiblePlaces.com

THE PEOPLE OF JUDAH WERE FOUND TO BE "ROTTEN GRAPES."

JESUS DESCRIBES THE PRUNING OF VINES AS THE
PROCESS OF CUTTING OFF THE FRUITLESS BRANCHES AND
CUTTING BACK THE FRUIT-BEARING BRANCHES.

*must remain in the vine. Neither can you bear fruit unless you remain
in me.*

*"I am the vine; you are the branches. If you remain in me and I in
you, you will bear much fruit; apart from me you can do nothing." (John
15:1–5)*

The Lord's followers were familiar with the image of the
divine Gardner, working in his vineyard to produce fruit. But
Jesus took their theological imagination in a new direction. He
identifies himself here not as the Gardener (his Father), but as
the vine. Though earlier "I am" statements in John equate the
Father and the Son, in this final claim Jesus constructs a cor-
relation between himself and God's people, historically understood as God's vine.[11] In a nuanced version of the ancient image,
Jesus locates his disciples as branches united to him. God now in
Christ has a faithful and fruitful vine. His disciples have only to
"remain in him" to bear fruit. The psalmist had long before predicted restoration for Israel through the Son of Man, who would
embody a new Israel (Ps. 80:14–19).

The parable in John 15 draws on more associations from the
world of vinedressers to make its points. Jesus' hearers knew
the vine sent out long, leafy shoots from its branches each year.

Such growth extends the vine up to ten times its length, but the tendrils must be cut back to ensure the vitality of the vine and its fruit. Jesus distinguishes between fruitless branches (those that do not "remain" in him) that are cut *off*,[12] and the fruit-bearing branches that are cut *back*. Pruning is described as the "cleansing" of unwanted shoots whose only real value is as firewood. Without this process, a vine is weakened. Greenery is traded for fruit.

John 15 brings together vineyard elements we have seen in our brief survey of divine gardening: selection, tending, intimacy, and fruit-bearing. Explaining the parable, Jesus says, "You did not choose me, but I chose you and appointed you so that you might go and bear fruit — fruit that will last — and so that whatever you ask in my name the Father will give you. This is my command: Love each other" (John 15:16 – 17). "Remaining" in Jesus is a unique way of referring to intimacy. Only those branches that are joined in life-giving union with the Vine and his words can produce the fruit that is love for others. Jesus invites the disciples into the intimacy he shares with the Father. No contemporary urban or technological image could capture the organic union that Jesus describes here so well.

Garden and vine imagery in the Bible has opened up insight into the closeness God desires with his people. Prophetic oracles and parables reveal the divine Farmer's passion and perplexity. God is determined to regain the fellowship we renounced in Eden. By making himself the Vine, Jesus ensures a faithful covenant partner in union with the Farmer. Now the Vinedresser asks us to maintain the intimacy that leads to fruitfulness — a fruitfulness that comes not by effort, but by submission to his provision and discipline.

Faith and the Divine Farmer

Having returned from a year of study in Israel in 2004, I decided to plant four grape vines in my yard, complete with a cedar trellis over which they could shoot their tendrils. I tended these vines for the next few years, watching them gain enormous growth each summer. I diligently pruned the branches back to strengthen the trunk and encourage

A SINGLE GARDENING EXPLOIT OPENED A WINDOW ON THE HEART OF GOD

fruitfulness. For reasons unknown to me, one vine died in each of the following years. Disease took them along with beetles that came by the hundreds. But my last vine stayed strong for some time. By itself, it covered the trellis each year. We even dined under it as an ancient Israelite might during the Feast of Tabernacles.

Then, the last vine died.

The skeletal trellis at the edge of our property stands as a reminder that my dream of a thriving "vineyard" required the combination of my competence and the collaboration of the vine.

A single gardening exploit opened a window on the heart of God: his diligence in planning, his commitment to nurture and prune, his expectancy for fruit-bearing, his desire for intimacy, his disappointment over fruitlessness, and his ultimate solution to guarantee success.

Chapter 4

THE DIVINE MONARCH AND HIS REGENTS

MAYBE FOR you the notion of royalty summons images of legendary rulers such as Queen Elizabeth or King Arthur. Or it may conjure mental pictures of impotent current-day figure-heads in ceremonial garb presiding over pompous occasions. The global grief over the sudden death of Princess Diana in August, 1997—the tragic end of a public life marked by relent-less public interest—betrays a resilient interest with royal dignitaries. This obsession was all the more obvious as Diana's coverage in the media overshadowed the response to Mother Theresa's passing less than a week later.

The rise of democracy has dented the almost universal tradition of permanently sanctioned royal dynasties. Though kings and princes still oversee countries in our modern world, we tend to find fawning over them at least surprising and often embarrassing. I admit that I am cynical when I see portraits of monarchs hanging in the windows of every shop and office in countries where these traditions continue. I cannot help but wonder how voluntary these uniform displays of adulation are.

In biblical times, however, this notion of human monarchy

RAMESES II AT THE ABU SIMBEL TEMPLE IN EGYPT.
© Franz Marc Frei/agefotostock

was virtually the only option imaginable. Israel, in fact, found it difficult to live exclusively under the reign of an invisible God. They envied "all the other nations" that had human kings (1 Sam. 8:5). If our journey into this world is effective, we will find ourselves with a renewed sense of awe for the God who reigns supreme over all creation and history and a refreshed sense of responsibility to serve God as his royal representatives on earth. This chapter will give us a chance to pick up a final layer of meaning to the notion of being made in God's image.

Ancient Kings, Wise and Mighty

The Hebrew term for king, *melek*, refers to rulers of every size "kingdom." Some were no more than sheiks of family clans. Others were truly imperial rulers. The biblical record is witness to the rise and fall of major empires, such as Egypt, Assyria, Babylon, Persia, Greece, and Rome. Regardless of the constituency, *melek* (used more than 2,700 times in the Old Testament!), implied absolute and sole authority over a kingdom. Ancient kings were depicted as judges and generals, as architects and sages. Their rule was often accompanied by great displays of wealth, the centralization of power (through taxation and land ownership), ritual activities, monumental building projects, and the waging of wars for both defense

© Faith Kocyildir/www.BigStockPhoto.com

THE PYRAMIDS ARE AN OBVIOUS EXAMPLE OF THE STRENGTH, POWER, AND WEALTH THAT THE ANCIENT KINGS WANTED TO PORTRAY.

and expansion. A widespread tendency to conceive of kings as divine beings (at least after death) characterized the ancient world. The very institution of kingship was presumed to be a gift from the gods.

Rule had both an internal and external focus. Within the kingdom, the monarch would rule as judge through the use of wise laws. King Hammurabi, ruler of Babylon during the time period of the patriarchs, introduced his law code with a divinely sanctioned mandate: "to promote the welfare of the people . . . to cause justice to prevail in the land . . . that the strong might not oppress the weak."[13] Through laws such as "an eye for an eye," rulers portrayed themselves as wise social architects, constructing and maintaining a just society where order and well-being prevailed. Social regulation in Egypt was called *maʾat*, named after the goddess of law, truth, balance, morality, justice, and order.

Similar notions were present throughout the Near East, including the Hebrew concept of *mišpāṭ* in the Old Testament. Usually translated "righteousness," this term can include the executive, legislative, and judicial aspects of governance, altogether best understood as *the alignment of society with God's will*. It shouldn't come as any surprise, then, that Israel's "judges" (a term from the same root) exercised royal functions. Moses, like Hammurabi, was laying the groundwork for a just and stable society through the laws of the Torah.

Baker Photo Archive, courtesy of the Louvre

HAMMURABI'S CODE

*See, I have taught you decrees and laws as the L*ORD *my God commanded me, so that you may follow them in the land you are entering to
take possession of it. Observe them carefully, for this will show your wisdom and understanding to the nations, who will hear about all these
decrees and say, "Surely this great nation is a wise and understanding
people." What other nation is so great as to have their gods near them
the way the L*ORD *our God is near us whenever we pray to him? And what
other nation is so great as to have such righteous decrees and laws as
this body of laws I am setting before you today? (Deut. 4:5–8)*

The other nations would also ask what kind of god dwelled
with this orderly community.

The external focus of royal rule was expressed by the
domination of outside forces. We will discuss the subject of
war directly in the next chapter. Here we focus on the importance of *maintaining* rule through treaties or covenants. Once
an enemy's threats were brought under control, the victorious
king would create a treaty between ruler and servant, called a
suzerain/vassal treaty. Treaties from across the ancient Near East combined the following conventional elements: (1) identification of the parties, (2) historical sum-mary of their relationship, (3) terms for proper relationship in the future (e.g., protection for the vassal and tribute for the suzerain), (4) consequences for keeping/

THE EGYPTIAN GOD MA'AT, REPRESENTING
LAW, ORDER, BALANCE, AND JUSTICE.

breaking the terms, (5) calling of witnesses (often divine), (6) notice regarding the covenant document, and (7) terms for renewal. Covenant-making ceremonies were sealed by the blood of an animal.

While all of these elements are not present in every treaty, they are in many and, most significantly, they are clearly evident in the biblical covenant that God made with his people on Mount Sinai. Yahweh (the covenant name for God) engaged his people through a familiar institution that reinforced his wisdom and sovereignty.

KING OF KINGS

The idea of Yahweh as Israel's divine king was completely intuitive in the world of the Old Testament. Every nation had deities in their pantheon, with one designated as the "patron" deity. For example, according to the Babylonian myth *Enuma Elish*, Marduk became the premier god of Babylon to whom all other gods chant, "O Marduk, you are the most important among the great gods . . . your command is supreme."[14] Marduk receives this praise as the one who had demonstrated his prowess over the threatening deities in the story. With joy the gods present him with scepter, throne, and staff, and they hail him as king.

The royal reign of God in the Bible is officially first announced on the heels of the Egyptians' defeat. In joyous song Moses and Miriam led Israel in their confession (Ex. 15:18). As their

ENUMA ELISH

WITH THE ISRAELITES' ESCAPE FROM EGYPT, GOD
DEMONSTRATED HIS POWER OVER PHARAOH
AND ALL THE GODS OF EGYPT.

rescuer, Yahweh had demonstrated that he was the legitimate
king of Israel and had the right to rule them. But he had also
proven that he was king over Pharaoh and all the deities of Egypt.

He is the King of kings!

God's kingship becomes a central theme in Israel's worship.
A specific group of hymns are called "enthronement" psalms
because they, like the song of Moses and Miriam, celebrate the
reign of God using the verb *mālak* (formed from the same root
in *melek*). In all, the Psalms mention God's royal rule more
than sixty-eight times. From both heaven and Mount Zion, God
reigns over all the nations and all their kings, beginning with
the king of Israel (Ps. 48:2).

> God reigns over the nations;
>> God is seated on his holy throne.
> The nobles of the nations assemble
>> as the people of the God of Abraham,
> for the kings of the earth belong to God;
>> he is greatly exalted. (Ps. 47:8–9)

They must bring him tribute (Ps. 96:8). The psalmist expects
the kings and peoples of the earth to join the forces of nature in
praise of God (Ps. 98).

FINDING THE LOST IMAGES OF GOD

In other parts of Scripture we find God humbling kings who, like Pharaoh, see themselves as divine rulers. Judgment came to the conceited king of Tyre because he boasted: "I am a god; I sit on the throne of a god in the heart of the seas" (Ezek. 28:2). The Assyrian king Sennacherib claimed divine sanction for his rule over all other kings. Taunting the puny Judean ruler after the northern kingdom had fallen, Sennacherib's envoy shouted for all to hear:

> "Do not let Hezekiah mislead you when he says, 'The LORD will deliver us.' Have the gods of any nations ever delivered their lands from the hand of the king of Assyria? Where are the gods of Hamath and Arpad? Where are the gods of Sepharvaim? Have they rescued Samaria from my hand? Who of all the gods of these countries have been able to save their lands from me? How then can the LORD deliver Jerusalem from my hand?" (Isa. 36:18–20)

Hezekiah knew what to pray: "Now, LORD our God, deliver us from his hand, *so that all the kingdoms of the earth may know that you, LORD, are the only God*" (Isa. 37:20, emphasis added). In response to this personal insult, God responded with a death blow to 185,000 Assyrian troops (Isa. 37:36).

One final example comes from Babylonian king Nebuchadnezzar, known widely as "king

ASSYRIAN KING SENNACHERIB WITH A ENUCH FOLLOWING BEHIND.

Baker Photo Archive, courtesy of the Pergamon Museum

RECONSTRUCTION OF THE
IMPRESSIVE ISHTAR GATE, BUILT BY
NEBUCHADNEZZAR.

of kings" (Ezek. 26:7). Daniel interpreted a foreboding dream for the self-deluded monarch: Nebuchadnezzar would act like a wild animal, eating grass like cattle. Seven years would pass until the arrogant king humbled himself and acknowledged the true God (Dan. 4:24–25). After the prediction comes true, the humbled king "praised the Most High; I honored and glorified him who lives forever. *His dominion is an eternal dominion; his kingdom endures from generation to generation*" (Dan. 4:34, emphasis added). These are the appropriate sentiments for any human ruler—though they don't come naturally.

Before we leave Daniel's dreams, we should notice an interesting figure that appears.

> *In my vision at night I looked, and there before me was one like a son of man, coming with the clouds of heaven. He approached the Ancient of Days and was led into his presence. He was given authority, glory and sovereign power; all nations and peoples of every language worshiped him. His dominion is an* everlasting dominion *that will not pass away, and his kingdom is one that will never be destroyed.* (Dan. 7:13–14, emphasis added)

Somehow, in this book that definitively puts human kings in their place beneath the King of kings, Daniel is given a glimpse of a humanlike figure who receives all the attributes of eternal dominion. To understand this more fully, we need to go back to Genesis and pick up another story line.

SON(S) OF GOD

When God created Adam and Eve, they were made "in his image," a phrase to which we have given some thought in chapter 2. Now it's time to dig deeper into the *royal* context of this passage. Here's what follows: "Fill the earth and *subdue it. Rule* over . . . every living creature" (Gen. 1:28, emphasis added). Ruling was inherent in the notion of being image-bearers. Kings in the ancient world often displayed physical images as symbolic representations of their continued sovereignty over a region in their absence. God had appointed Adam and Eve as his "regents," in charge of extending his order and rule throughout the world. The psalmist restates this status:

TIGLATH-PILESER III SHOWN WITH AN ENEMY UNDER HIS FOOT. IT WAS COMMON TO DEPICT A DEFEATED ENEMY UNDER THE FEET OF THE RULER.

Aerial shot of Megiddo, one of the three cities that Solomon fortified. Solomon increased the size of his father's kingdom and gathered many riches and many wives. Unfortunately, soon after, the kingdom was split in two.

> *Yet you made [man] a little lower than the heavenly beings*
>   *and crowned him with glory and honor.*
> *You have given him dominion over the works of your hands;*
>   *you put all things under his feet,*
> *all sheep and oxen,*
>   *and also the beasts of the field,*
> *the birds of the heavens, and the fish of the sea,*
>   *whatever passes along the paths of the seas. (Ps. 8:4 – 8 ESV,*
>   *emphasis added)*

This inspired worldview locates humans at the intersection of earth and heaven—at the place where kings alone supposedly sat. Competing myths in antiquity reinforced a socially stratified society with godlike qualities reserved for monarchs, often called the "son of God." But in the Bible that place is reserved *for all of us!* We all trace our lineage back to Adam, the first "son of God" (Luke 3:38).

Though the first humans were, amazingly, "like God" (Gen. 1:26), they were, more importantly, *not* God. The devil pushed them toward the sin that characterized his own rebellion—the effort to replace God with ourselves (Isa. 14:13 – 14). Human hubris is as ironic for us as it is for Satan. God gave us a unique role as his regents over creation, but in grasping for greater power, we lose our souls. The oracle against the king of Tyre in Ezekiel is followed by a lament for him in Eden! The prophet understood that the pride of Adam beat in the heart of the Tyrian king. He, too, was removed from the splendor and bounty he once enjoyed (Ezek. 28:11 – 19).

As God's people, we struggle to reconcile God's ultimate rule and our royal-but-subordinate role. I find this to be one of the biggest challenges leaders face today, and you can trace it through Scripture. Having rescued Israel from Egypt, Moses declared, "God reigns." On Mount Sinai God summoned his people to live as a "*kingdom* of priests" or a "*royal* priesthood" (Ex. 19:6). They were, *as a people* (like Pharaoh), called God's son (Ex. 4:23). But in Moses' final words to the son ready to take his inheritance, he warned Israel about the desire for a human king. Assuming the inevitability of a monarch, he established numerous restraints. In spite of these measures, Moses remained pessimistic about the outcome (Deut. 17).

Gideon's son Abimelek (whose name means "my father is king") staged the nation's first attempt at kingship. God had shown Gideon that victory over the Midianites would result from divine intervention alone. Following the battle the people asked Gideon to rule over them, to which he wisely responded, "I will not rule over you, nor will my son rule over you. *The* Lord *will rule over you*" (Judg. 8:23, emphasis added). In the next chapter Abimelek tried to establish himself as ruler—and failed miserably.

Later the whole tribal confederation would demand a king. In a dialogue between Samuel and the divine King, God conceded the nation's request as a rejection of his own kingship. Yet he instructed Samuel to provide Israel with what they wanted, though without relinquishing the supreme role as Israel's divine King (1 Sam. 12:12 – 13). King Saul's reign ushered in no improvement over life under the judges. And even though David was a king "after [God's] own heart," he too fell into the trap of royal pretense and presumption (2 Sam. 11 and 24). Solomon turned out to be "Exhibit A" for all of Moses' predictions (Deut. 17:16 – 17; 1 Kings 10:23 – 29; 11:1 – 4; 12:4). He gathered horses and chariots, multiplied wives through political marriages,

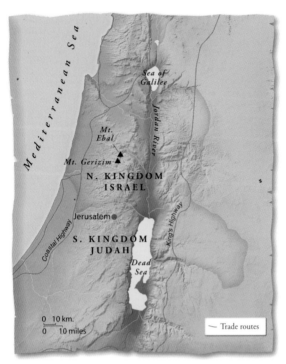

THE DIVIDED KINGDOM

and put himself above his brothers ... even, perhaps, God. It's rather telling that his palace took almost twice as long to build as God's temple! Soon the kingdom split in two. Eventually both kingdoms suffered horrific destruction and exile.

As we examine this history, we must not miss God's choice to establish a monarchy in Israel *anyway*. Through this choice he was continuing a long-term plan to assure the permanence of his own reign. God promised David that he would have a son perpetually on his throne (2 Sam. 7:16). Solomon, the first to inherit this promise, was to be a son of God (2 Sam. 7:14). This covenant with David is celebrated in royal psalms that use "son of God" language to refer to the anointed king (Ps. 2:7). God's "royal son" in Psalm 72 will bring prosperity (v. 7) and will receive tribute from the nations who bow down to him (vv. 10−11). A messianic, or "anointed," line was thereby established leading directly to Jesus: from the *Son of David* ... to the *Son of God*.

KING OF THE JEWS

At the time of Jesus' birth, the Roman Empire—and the rule of the Caesars—dominated the world. With Caesar Augustus, "the revered one," came the tradition of associating emperors with the gods while alive and declaring them fully divine after death. An imperial cult of emperor worship ensued. Augustus

THE ROMAN EMPIRE

and his successors used titles from former empires such as "Son of God" and "King of kings."

In first-century Palestine, a local megalomaniac grasped for power. "Herod the Great" made his way to the Roman Senate to be named "king of the Jews." Although he undertook a decades-long reconstruction of the Jewish temple, Herod was hated by those he ruled, including family members who were at risk of assassination. This was the Herod of Matthew 2, who killed all the male children under two years of age because word came of a rival king's birth. Not surprisingly, most New Testament references to "kings

CAESAR AUGUSTUS

HEROD BUILT THE MAGNIFICENT PORT ON THE MEDITERRANEAN SEA TO HONOR AND WELCOME THE ROMAN CAESAR. HE NAMED IT CAESAREA.

of the earth" (or of "Gentiles" or "the whole world") are negative (see Matt. 17:25). These are the rulers who abused their authority and lorded it over the people (Mark 10:42).

Enter Jesus Christ.

The title "Christ," used well over five hundred times in the New Testament, means "anointed one." As a baby, Jesus was honored by mysterious Magi from the East and prophetic prayers that welcomed him as Israel's long-awaited deliverer (Matt. 2:1–12; Luke 1:68–75; 2:30–32, 38). At his baptism God called him "my Son, whom I love" (Luke 3:22), a clear authentication of his

THE EVENTS SURROUNDING JESUS' BIRTH AND BAPTISM CONFIRM HIS "ROYAL" STATUS.

FINDING THE LOST IMAGES OF GOD

royal status. He is called Son of David by the sick and the Son of God by demons (Matt. 9:27; 8:29). Mark introduced his gospel with Jesus as the Son of God (1:1) and ended it with a centurion confessing, "Surely this man was the Son of God!" (15:39). At the end of his life Jesus was charged by the Jews for blasphemy because he identified himself as Daniel's divine Son of Man (Mark 14:62–64), and he was crucified by the Romans as the self-proclaimed "King of the Jews" (Matt. 27:11–37).

While the identity of Jesus as God's anointed one was validated by his resurrection, only in the visions of Revelation is global recognition of him as "King of kings and Lord of lords" achieved (Rev. 19:16). Only at the end of history as we know it will the "kingdom of the world" be again "the kingdom of our Lord and of his Messiah, and he will reign for ever and ever" (Rev. 11:15). Until that full, eternal realization of his reign, we are witnesses to his legitimate sovereignty as members of his inaugurated kingdom. We "say among the nations, 'The LORD reigns'" (Ps. 96:10).

THE KINGDOM OF GOD AND HIS STEWARDS

The true identity of Christ is reinforced by the central focus of his teaching on the kingdom of God (or heaven).[15] Terms for "kingdom" appear more than one hundred times in Matthew, Mark, and Luke. Jesus, like John the Baptist, called people to repent, for the kingdom was "at hand" (Matt. 3:2 KJV). The long-awaited liberation of God's people was arriving. This was the "gospel" (lit., "good news"). Jesus invited people to "enter" the kingdom by living under the reign of God (see Matt. 5:20).

The kingdom of God is prominent in many of Jesus' parables. These profoundly simple stories reinforce a vision of God as a benevolent, patient, and generous king who sometimes hosts a lavish banquet (Matt. 22:1–14). This kingdom also serves as the context for reward and judgment (25:14–30). Parables involving tenants or stewards were warnings to the religious leaders of his day. Most had betrayed the trust they were given as rulers in the community (Luke 19:12–27). In Matthew 18:23–35 they responded to the king's mercy by heaping revenge on others.

Stewardship is another way of describing what we referred

IN THE GREAT VISIONS OF REVELATION, THE
LAMB ASSUMES HIS PLACE AT HIS THRONE.

to as regency. Joseph, for example, had been one of Pharaoh's
regents. He was put in charge because God was with him and
he could be trusted as a "Number 2" (Gen. 41:38–40). In the
parables, faithful stewardship is expected of those entrusted
with vineyards or monetary resources in the king's absence. In
Christ, God was coming back to check on his trustees. Rather
than proving their allegiance, some chose to kill the Son in
open defiance (Matt. 21:38).

Jesus' trustworthy disciples will be rewarded for following him as their king. In the great visions of Revelation, the
Lamb assumes his place at the center of the throne. The living
creatures sing a song that recalls the ancient identity of God's
people:

> *You are worthy . . . because you were slain,*
> *and with your blood you purchased for God*
> *persons from every tribe and language and people and*
> *nation.*
> *You have made them to be a kingdom and priests to serve*
> *our God,*

and they will reign on the earth. *(Rev. 5:9 – 10, emphasis added)*

Only witnesses to the supreme rule of Christ are eligible to serve as his eternal regents.

FAITH AND THE DIVINE MONARCH

Perhaps modern monarchy and royal despots deserve our cynicism. The saying is true: "Power corrupts and absolute power corrupts absolutely." The Bible offers a sustained critique of the human tendency to lose sight of divine rule. I wonder, however, if the capacity to appreciate our King's majestic splendor has been diminished by our modern sensibilities.

Our songs of worship have the right words. We verbally exalt the King of all kings.

The challenge is to live completely under his reign as we prepare for an eternity of service and praise.

Chapter 5

THE DIVINE WARRIOR AND HIS ARMY

ONE SPRING morning in 2004 I dropped our children off at their "Ulpan," a Hebrew immersion program in Jerusalem. On the way back to the other side of the city I heard an explosion and almost immediately saw a man running toward my line of traffic waving us away. Another bus was blown up in the "Holy City." A self-detonating radical added to a cycle of violence that seems ever more intractable. The grief in the "Middle East Conflict" never ends.

Some say history is hardly more than the history *of war*. Certainly this appears to be the case in the history of the Middle East. The cycle of sacked cities, destroyed infrastructure, exiled captives, and reconfigured dominion constitutes the backdrop for most of Scripture. War is, of course, an ever-present global reality. It touches all of us. In the last century alone, more than 150 million lives were lost to war and genocide. In many parts of the world only the rare family is untouched by the loss of life or limb and the seething emotion of revenge-seeking bitterness. Recent American wars from Vietnam to Iraq have provoked deep debate. For many, war is a

CAPTIVES BEING EXILED FROM LACHISH BY ASSYRIAN KING
SENNACHERICB (7TH CENT. BC).

necessary evil, symptomatic of a fallen world. For others, it is—
potentially—a noble undertaking. Sentiments about war and
warriors range from horror to honor.

The Bible chronicles war as a major recurring fact of
human history. It also engages military imagery as a central,
root metaphor to describe the work of God and his people.
From the startling statement in Exodus 15:3 that God is a
"warrior" to Revelation's final, catastrophic battle, the "LORD of
hosts" (ESV language) is fully engaged in epic conflict. History is indeed the history of war, but human combat is only an
echo of an eternally significant engagement. A larger battle
of cosmic scope is raging. The stakes in this war are much
higher.

Every creature on earth, heaven, and hell is inescapably
involved.

So please venture with me into this topic carefully. We are
rightfully horrified by the atrocities of war. Suicide bombers
engaging "holy war" threaten to destabilize the civilized world.
Our media glorifies violence. Somehow, we must find a way to
appreciate the imagery of warfare in the Bible in a way that is
edifying and not destructive.

Cosmic Warfare

The first fully descriptive account of a divinely sponsored battle follows the Israelite exodus from Egypt. Moses had repeatedly challenged the resistant ruler of Egypt on Yahweh's behalf to free the people. God's sequence of plagues systematically demolished Egypt's mythology, culminating with the death of the "divine" heir to the throne. Loaded with spoils of gold, the Israelites headed to the holy mountain of Yahweh. In one last confrontation, Pharaoh pursued Israel to face again the powers of their strange God. In the Sea of Reeds Yahweh drowned Pharaoh's armies — and any hope of recapturing the renegade slaves.

Two side-by-side reports of this victory identify this as the supernatural, militant intervention of God. The Egyptians in the narrative account say, "Let's get away from the Israelites! *The* Lord *is fighting for them against Egypt*" (Ex. 14:25, emphasis added). Exodus 15 is more poetic:

THE EXODUS ROUTE OF THE ISRAELLITES

PHARAOH'S CHARIOTS BEING HURLED INTO THE SEA DEPICTED IN THE PAINTING BY BERNARDINO LUINI (C.1475-1532).

> The LORD is a warrior;
>> the LORD is his name.
> Pharaoh's chariots and his army
>> he has hurled into the sea.
> The best of Pharaoh's officers
>> are drowned in the Red Sea.
> The deep waters have covered them;
>> they sank to the depths like a stone. (Ex. 15:3–5, emphasis
>> added)

The king who said, "Who is the LORD, that I should obey him and let Israel go? I do not know the LORD" (Ex. 5:2), would succumb to the power of this unknown divine Warrior.

Cosmic dimensions of the conflict with Pharaoh resurface in other biblical passages. Notice references to mythical sea creatures in Psalm 74:

> But God is my King from long ago;
>> he brings salvation on the earth.
> It was you who split open the sea by your power;
>> you broke the heads of the monster in the waters.
> It was you who crushed the heads of Leviathan
>> and gave it as food to the creatures of the desert.
> It was you who opened up springs and streams;
>> you dried up the ever-flowing rivers.
> (Ps. 74:12–15, emphasis added; see also Ps. 89:8–10)

This testimony of the Almighty's rule over the sea and his defeat of its creatures challenged the creation myths of the ancient world. In alternative renditions, the watery chaos, often known as "the Sea," was viewed as a divinity. In the Psalms, however, God conquered these forces at creation (Ps. 74:16; 89:11). Biblically, then, the victory over Egypt was an echo of a cosmological victory won at the beginning of the world. This war on earth took place in tandem with a long-standing battle in the heavens.

Turn the scrolls back to the garden of Eden, where a diabolical serpent challenged the plan of the Lord. In response, God vowed, "I will put enmity between you and the woman, and between your offspring and hers; *he will crush your head, and you will strike his heel*" (Gen. 3:15, emphasis added). This serpent, like Leviathan and Rahab, engaged ensuing generations in combat by empowering imposter regimes that defied the true Lord. Rahab refers to the Nile crocodile and, by extension, to arrogant Egypt (Isa. 30:7). God cut this monster to pieces (Isa. 51:9; cf. Job 26:12) so that, like Babylon and other demonically inspired empires, it would acknowledge the one true God (Ps. 87:4).

Holy War

Before Israel's divine Warrior overran the Egyptians in battle, he made a remarkable promise: "The LORD will fight for you; you need only to be still" (Ex. 14:14). Israel's role as *believing spectators* reminds us that the ultimate war is unseen. When the Israelites engaged in their first battle in the Promised Land, God "gave" them the city of Jericho (Josh. 6:16). Before this miracle, Israel's commander, Joshua, had an alarming encounter with an armed figure with drawn sword. "Are you for us or for our enemies?" he asked. "Neither," came the reply, "but as *commander of the army of the LORD* I have now come" (Josh. 5:13–14). Joshua—whose name means "Yahweh delivers"—came face to face with his heavenly counterpart leading the armies of God.

The armies or "hosts of the LORD" are regularly mentioned in the Bible, most often in the title "the LORD of hosts." David defied Goliath and the Philistine armies by appealing to "the

JOSHUA'S DESTRUCTION AT JERICHO, BASED ON PAINTING BY ROBERT LEINWEBER.

LORD of hosts, the God of the armies of Israel" (1 Sam 17:45 NRSV). He knew that the odds on the ground were nothing compared to the odds in the invisible world. Elisha perceived that an army of Arameans surrounding him was nothing compared to the temporarily visible flaming horses and chariots of God (2 King 6:8–23). King Jehoshaphat was encouraged before a vast human army not to be dismayed, "for the battle is not yours, but God's.... You will not have to fight this battle. Take up your positions; *stand firm and see the deliverance the Lord will give you*" (2 Chron. 20:15, 17, emphasis added). Throughout Scripture God is pictured as an all-powerful conquering Warrior whose victories on heaven and earth are enjoyed and experienced by believers who stand in faith and watch. As Paul would later say, "If God is for us, who can be against us?" (Rom. 8:31).

A concept of "holy war" was widely shared in the ancient world. Most ethnic or national groups assumed that their gods fought with them and for them. Israel's beliefs were different. The families that came out of Egypt were transformed into a spiritual militia in the desert (Num. 1:2–3). God drafted this earthly army to destroy the Amorites, who were in total rebellion against him. The "sin of the Amorites" had reached full measure in Canaan, and God mobilized his troops to remove these trespassers (Gen. 15:16). They were to engage in *ḥērem*, the total dedication of persons or property to God—in this case by destruction.

God demanded this ritual destruction from Joshua's armies at Jericho. To ignore the command was to fail to attribute public victory to their divine Warrior. Just as importantly, Israel needed to acknowledge that God was the ultimate judge of human misconduct in the Promised Land. Achan learned that an Israelite could become the object of God's judgment as easily as a Canaanite. He and his family were permanently enshrined, like Jericho, in a pile of stones (Josh. 7:26). Prophets routinely warned Israel about the precarious nature of serving in God's army.

Let me emphasize here that Israel's mandate to wage war in Canaan was a unique form of divine punishment for sin that had been entrenched there for centuries (Gen. 15:16). They were *instruments* of God's wrath who, after breaking faith with God, would later became the *objects* of his wrath. The book of Joshua by no means sets a precedent for genocide, a sick reality with catastrophic carnage. History is punctuated by countless wars in the name of God. The biblical conquest was rather one of many exceptional occasions, like the flood, when God brought the punishment of sin dramatically into human experience. As our discussion progresses, we will discover that God prefers to take this judgment on himself. In doing so, he sets us free from revenge and hatred.

A MILITANT MESSIAH AND A NEW CONQUEST

Fast forward fifteen centuries to the time of the New Testament. The Gospels begin with two conflicting social realities in ancient Palestine: oppressive Roman occupation and persistent Jewish aspirations for liberation. Jewish hope took the form of frequent uprisings that were often led by "messianic" figures such as Simon, a former slave of Herod; the shepherd Athronges; and Judas of Galilee, one of the founders of the Zealot sect.

Though some modern readers think of Jesus as a nonmilitant figure, the Gospels present a more complex profile. Luke's gospel begins with provocative prayers of praise for a coming liberator. Mary glorified the Lord for scattering the proud and toppling rulers (Luke 1:51–52). Zechariah blessed the Lord for the horn of salvation—"salvation from our enemies and from the hand of all who hate us" (Luke 1:71). The angelic announcement to the shepherds in Luke 2 came with terrifying glory (2:9) and the sudden appearance of "a great company of the heavenly host" (v. 13). These are the "hosts" we met in the conquest, the armies of God who stand ready to serve their celestial Captain. On the day his formal ministry began in Nazareth, Jesus claimed that the following words of Isaiah were spoken of him: "The Spirit of the Lord . . . has sent me . . . to set the oppressed free, to proclaim the year of the Lord's favor" (Luke 4:18–19).

Prior to this announcement Jesus faced his real enemy in the wilderness: Satan, the serpent from Genesis 3. The predicted confrontation in the garden of Eden resurfaced. The devil tempted Jesus three times, trying to sidetrack him from his mission. Yet Jesus refused to bargain with the temporary ruler of this world. Satan lost in this attempt, but he determined, ominously, to return at "an opportune time" (Luke 4:13).

A final battle would settle the score.

Though Satan is not mentioned again until Passion Week,

THE WILDERNESS IN WHICH JESUS WAS TEMPTED BY SATAN.

© 1995 Phoenix Data Systems

FINDING THE LOST IMAGES OF GOD

JESUS COMMANDING DEMONS OUT OF A MAN
AND INTO THE HERD OF SWINE.

his demonic armies rallied as their messianic counterpart
became more militant. Mark's gospel begins the account of
Jesus' ministry by recording the screams of a demonized man:
"What do you want with us, Jesus of Nazareth? *Have you come
to destroy us?*" (Mark 1:23–24, emphasis added). Exorcisms
punctuate the teaching ministry of Jesus and the gathering of
his spiritual militia (3:15).

Mark tells us that one day after Jesus had been teaching
near the lake, he said, "Let us go over to the other side" (Mark
4:35). "The other side" may reflect a traditional Jewish expression for that which goes unnamed. Jesus brought them to the
eastern side of the Sea of Galilee, the *Gentile* side associated
with *Roman* rule and its *pagan* lifestyle. As they approached the
land of their spiritual enemies, a violent storm erupted. Such
storms—what Mark calls a "furious squall" (4:37)—result
from winds that rush from the east, churning up swells of
six to eight feet. They terrify fishermen to this day. Yet Jesus
was asleep at the rudder. The trembling disciples shook Jesus
awake only to watch him rebuke the wind and turn the sea to
glass. Stunned, they asked, "Who is this? Even the wind and
the waves obey him!" (4:41).

Their rabbi was beginning to reveal his true identity and mission. Only God had power to command the stormy seas. That was made clear in a former battle with the cosmic forces at the Sea of Reeds. Like his human namesake Joshua, Jesus (pronounced *Jeshua* in Hebrew) was leading his army into battle. Waiting on the other side of the lake was a demonized man, held captive by unclean spirits and too strong for any human to bind. Catching sight of Jesus he shouted, "What do you want with me, Jesus, Son of the Most High God? In God's name don't torture me!" (Mark 5:7). Jesus addressed the man, asking his name. "Legion," came the answer, using the name of a Roman military unit often comprising several thousand soldiers. Jesus commanded the spirits out, permitting them to enter a nearby herd of swine. Two thousand demon-possessed pigs promptly rushed off the hill and drowned in the sea (5:13).

The military imagery in these stories is unmistakable. The running boar was one of the mascots of the tenth Roman Legion—the legion that would sack Jerusalem in AD 70. Though naturally good swimmers, the pigs, like Pharaoh's horses and chariots, sank into the depths. The divine Warrior's power overwhelmed them. However, the ultimate enemy was not Rome. Jesus defeated first the sea's storm and then freed a demonized man who lived among the dead. As in the exodus, God battled his ancient foe to reclaim human territory usurped by the devil.

A new conquest had begun.[16]

THE GATES OF HELL AND THE KEYS OF THE KINGDOM

The disciples found themselves on a journey of discovery regarding the military mission of their Messiah. Jesus sought to reshape their ideas about the war and their enemy. A choice place to teach them lay at the base of Mount Hermon in Caesarea Philippi. In Old Testament times this region sheltered at least fourteen temples dedicated to the storm god Baal. In the time of Jesus a Roman city was erected here. It boasted a white marble temple honoring Augustus and a great stone mound in which niches held statues venerating the nature god Pan. In this epicenter of paganism Jesus commissioned his disciples, declaring victory over everything that hell would hurl at them.

Jesus began his critical message with a question, "Who do people say the Son of Man is?" followed by a more personal one, "Who do *you* say I am?" (Matt. 16:13, 15, emphasis added). Peter spoke up: "You are the Messiah, the Son of the living God" (16:16). Jesus

The temple at Caesarea Philippi

blessed Peter for his response and pronounced: "You are Peter, and on this rock I will build my church, and the gates of Hades will not overcome it. I will give you the keys of the kingdom of heaven; whatever you bind on earth will be bound in heaven, and whatever you loose on earth will be loosed in heaven" (16:18–19).

The image of a rock has a double meaning. Peter's name means *rock* in both Aramaic (*Kepha*) and Greek (*Petros*). While Protestants and Roman Catholics debate whether the rock was Peter (suggesting the origins of apostolic succession) or his confession, an obvious historical sense is that the rock is Peter as the disciples' spokesperson and leader. He served as such throughout the Gospels and led them in opening the kingdom to Jews and Gentiles in Acts 2, 8, and 10.

The rocky outcropping where Jesus and his disciples likely stood contributes more symbolism. At the base of the mound

Wikimedia Commons

THE CAVE AT CAESAREA PHILIPPI WHICH GREEKS AND ROMANS BELIEVED LED TO THE UNDERWORLD.

sits a gaping cave where the underground springs could then be seen bubbling up. The dark cave emanated mythical associations with the powers of death. It was one of the "gates of Hades" that the Greeks and Romans believed led to the underworld.[17] Jesus might have deliberately chosen this place to stake a flag in the ground for his movement. He promised his warriors, "Nothing hell can do will stop you!"

The "gates of Hades" also referred to death itself. This connection leads us to Christ's next comments to the disciples. He pointed them to the cross. The great paradox of his mission now lay bare: *he would defeat death by dying* (Matt. 16:21).

Shocked and confused, Peter admonished his Master. Jesus saw the enemy behind his partially enlightened follower's outburst: "Get behind me Satan! You are a stumbling block to me" (Matt. 16:23). As the plan unfolded, so did the opposition. The devil had determined his opportune time.

The last hours of Christ's life were a pitched battle in a death-defying war fought without conventional weapons. "Put your sword back in its place," he ordered his companions (Matt. 26:52). As Lord of hosts, *Jeshua* could summon twelve legions of angels (26:53). But the Lamb of God would personally enter the gates of Hades to rescue humanity from the captivity of death. No wonder that at the crucifixion the earth trembled and the dead abandoned their graves (27:51–53)! A clear echo of Eden's prediction, Paul wrote, "He must reign until he has put all his enemies *under his feet*. The last enemy to be destroyed is

AT CHRIST'S CRUCIFIXION DARKNESS COVERED THE EARTH AND THE GROUND SHOOK, RELEASING THE DEAD FROM THEIR GRAVES.

Ms 65/1284 f.153r Darkness at the Death of Christ, from the Tres Riches Heures du Duc de Berry, early 15th century, Limbourg, Pol de (d.c.1416)/Musee Conde, Chantilly, France/The Bridgeman Art Library

death" (1 Cor. 15:25–26, emphasis added). The serpent who had stolen perpetual life from humanity in Eden was now robbed of his venom.

TAKING PRISONERS

Although the gospel accounts demonstrate a clear victory over Satan at Calvary, military engagement continues to be a way of life for the human army of God. On several occasions Paul assumed that his ministry was best understood with military metaphors. To the Corinthians Paul declared:

> *For though we live in the world, we do not wage war as the world does. The weapons we fight with are not the weapons of the world. On the contrary, they have divine power to demolish strongholds. We demolish arguments and every pretension that sets itself up against the knowledge of God, and we take captive every thought to make it*

obedient to Christ. And we will be ready to pun-ish every act of disobedience, once your obedi-ence is complete. (2 Cor. 10:3–6, emphasis added.)

REPLICA OF A ROMAN CATAPULT AT MASADA.

Paul's read-ers knew well the sequence of Roman warfare: lay siege, destroy fortifications, take captives, and punish resistance. In 146 BC Roman general Mum-mius defeated the Corinthians and turned the walls of their stronghold, the Acrocorinth, into rubble. They would also have under-stood the mind as a battle-ground, a metaphor common among the philosophers of the day. Paul recognized the real enemy as the devil, the originator of all deviant theology (2 Cor. 2:11; 11:3). In the spirit of the messianic Liberator, he intended to take captive such thinking and to free those enslaved to deceptive philosophy (11:3).

ROMAN SOLDIER TAKING A PRISONER CAPTIVE.

Avoiding smooth-talking heretics, they could anticipate Satan lying "crushed under [their] feet" (Rom. 16:20).

Paul was on the front lines in God's ongoing military engagement.

SCOURGING WAS A FORM OF ROMAN PUNISHMENT

GOD'S ARMOR

To prepare for the war, believers needed a protective suit of armor. Paul's letter to the Ephesians culminates with a solemn charge to wear God's armor:

Finally, be strong in the Lord and in his mighty power. Put on the full armor of God, so that you can take your stand against the devil's schemes. For our struggle is not against flesh and blood, but against the

THE ACROCORINTH, WHICH WAS THE STRONGHOLD FOR THE PEOPLE OF CORINTH.

ROMAN ARMOR

rulers, *against the authorities, against the powers of this dark world and against the spiritual forces of evil in the heavenly realms. Therefore put on the full armor of God, so that when the day of evil comes, you may be able to stand your ground, and after you have done everything, to stand. Stand firm then, with the belt of truth buckled around your waist, with the breastplate of righteousness in place, and with your feet fitted with the readiness that comes from the gospel of peace. In addition to all this, take up the shield of faith, with which you can extinguish all the flaming arrows of the evil one. Take the helmet of salvation and the sword of the Spirit, which is the word of God.* (Eph. 6:10–17)

The refrain to "take your stand," "stand your ground," and "stand firm" pictures the Roman tactic whereby soldiers locked themselves together side-by-side, facing their enemies. They remained impregnable only in this formation. The phrase recalls an Old Testament image of standing in faith and watching God fight for his people (Isa. 7:9). Interestingly, most of the gear mentioned in this passage evokes depictions of *God's* armor in Isaiah.[18] Our defense against dark powers is made up of *divine* qualities such as truth, righteousness, and faith, and the single offensive weapon of *God's* Word.

THE FINAL BATTLE

The Bible culminates in the apocalyptic images of Revelation. The final hours of this world's history will inspire the most heinous efforts of the devil (the "dragon" of Rev. 20:2) and his inspired kingdoms ("Babylon") to destroy God's chosen people. The dragon will war against "those who keep God's commands and hold fast their testimony about Jesus" (12:17).

A devil-empowered beast from the sea will deceive humanity (13:1–8).

In spite of Satan's destructive prowess, Jesus will triumph. As the "firstborn from the dead" who "hold[s] the keys of death and Hades" (1:5, 18), Jesus is shown with a double-edged sword jutting from his mouth (1:16). This image reminds us that God's Word is crucial to enduring the cosmic clash. This warrior, "the Lion of the tribe of Judah," appears in John's vision as "a Lamb, looking as if it had been slain" (5:6; cf. 13:8), worthy by his death to lead those who have suffered in his cause (6:9).

In John's vision "the great dragon . . . that ancient serpent called the devil, or Satan" (Rev. 12:9) is bound for a thousand years while martyrs for Christ are authorized as agents of justice (20:2, 4). Then the enemy wages a final battle to deceive and destroy God's people. After this, God throws the devil, death, and Hades into a lake of fire and replaces this world with a new heaven and earth—coming full circle in a story that began with creation.

REENACTMENT OF ROMAN SOLDIERS TAKING THEIR STAND, LOCKING TOGETHER SIDE-BY-SIDE.

THE FOUR HORSEMEN OF THE APOCALYPSE BY VICTOR MIKHAILOVICH (1848-1926). REVELATION TALKS ABOUT THE FINAL BATTLE WHEN GOD WILL OVERTHROW THE DEVIL.

FAITH AND THE DIVINE WARRIOR

Whether or not we have fought in war in its literal sense, we have no choice but to join forces in the cosmic battle that rages around us. Though Christ has won the war, we still battle unseen forces that will continue their assault until the final day.

There will be casualties.

There will be losses.

But we engage with the armor of God and with confidence in his ultimate victory.

John's vision holds out hope for all of us. Hope of a new world created for those who have fought and died with the Lamb. An eternal city without suffering and death. A new paradise without the diabolical serpent.

A new history without war.

FINDING THE LOST IMAGES OF GOD

Chapter 6

THE DIVINE
SHEPHERD AND
HIS FLOCK

ONE OF the most popular biblical images of God is the good Shepherd, epitomized in the parable of John 10 and that treasured passage, Psalm 23. Shepherds also feature as the primary metaphor for leaders in the Bible, an image we might miss because of the preference in Bible translations for the term "pastor" in the New Testament. Everyone who lived in the ancient Near East would have either lived in a household that owned flocks or seen the shepherds who led their sheep to graze along the edges of settled areas.

What comes to your mind when you think of sheep and shepherds? Those of us living in industrialized societies may think in overly sentimental pictures. A staff-holding, psalm-writing shepherd surrounded by a flock of peacefully resting sheep and goats. An occasional venture across verdant pastures to flowing streams. A leisurely life in a pastoral setting.

In my frequent visits with Bedouin shepherds in Jordan, I enter the timeless world of black goat-hair tents, herds of white "fat-tail" sheep, and the fireside hospitality that promises provision and protection. These shepherds struggle together

MIDDLE EASTERN SHEPHERD LEADING HIS FLOCK
Dr. Tim Laniak

EVERYONE IN THE ANCIENT NEAR EAST WOULD HAVE
OWNED FLOCKS OR SEEN THE SHEPHERDS WHO LED THEIR
SHEEP TO GRAZE ALONG THE EDGES OF SETTLED AREAS.

for their flocks' success in an inhospitable environment characterized by predators, precipices, and the constant threat of drought. One of the shepherds describes traces of wolves and hyenas in their camp. Out in the market another introduces a friend who always loses his sheep. Someone else will eventually return those he can't find. "These are good people," he

BEDOUIN SHEPHERD WITH HIS HERD AND TENT

FINDING THE LOST IMAGES OF GOD

THE SHEEP IN GREEN PASTURES WAS A COMMON IMAGE FOR A
LEADER'S COMPREHENSIVE NEED-MEETING

explains. I'm then invited for *mansaf*, a sumptuous meal of boiled goat on rice and bread. (If we're lucky, they'll serve it with brains and eyeballs!)[19]

The term *shepherd* was widely used in the ancient world for wise kings, and often for kings at war. It need not surprise us that shepherds like David were competent not only in poetry but also in hand-to-hand combat with wild beasts. We need to comprehend shepherding in its original context in order to fully appreciate Jesus who, in Revelation, is a militant, ruling Shepherd-Lamb. He provides for his flock *and* judges the nations.

THE SHEPHERD PSALM

Psalm 23 captures the essence of a day in the life of a shepherd. It begins with a short relational statement: "The LORD is my shepherd." In context, the whole sentence can be read, "*Because* the LORD is my shepherd, I lack nothing." The scenes of green pastures and still waters embellish the portrait of a shepherd who meets all the needs of his sheep. This comprehensive need-meeting in a wilderness setting requires skill, knowledge, and hard work (Jer. 3:15). Shepherds know that the same

GOOD SHEPERDS SEEK OUT WATER SOURCES IN AN ARID ENVIRONMENT.

SHEEP NEED A GOOD GUIDE SINCE TRAILS IN THE TERRAIN CAN BE MISLEADING.

skies withholding rain in one area dump it unexpectedly in another. Herders roam, searching for grasslands, aware that poisonous plants, relentless parasites, and venomous spiders threaten their flocks. Because water usually runs off the dry valley beds, good shepherds seek out collecting pools ("quiet waters"), where sheep can slake their thirst in peace. In these calm places, the divine Shepherd renews vitality or, more traditionally, "restores my soul" (NRSV).

"Leading" in verse 2 is followed by "guiding" along "right paths" in verse 3. The sheep need an attentive and knowledgeable guide to lead them through the myriad of dangerous narrow ruts in the terrain. This guidance is all the more important through the valley of deadly darkness (traditionally, "shadow of death"), when the sun begins to set and night blankets the desert valleys.

The Bible never makes the analogy that people are stupid like sheep. It does demonstrate awareness that both tend to wander. "Prone to wander, Lord, I feel it" goes the old hymn. Flocks of sheep tend to drift, often along dangerous paths. A few years ago a group of Turkish shepherds watched helplessly while 1,500 of their sheep walked off a cliff, simply because each one was following another. The one in front had wandered unknowingly along a trail that led to death and no shepherd was in front to direct their paths.

The choices in the desert require a faithful guide.

The divine Shepherd comforts the sheep because he has proven himself a reliable guard. His rod, a symbol of vigilant protection, and his staff, a symbol of care, reassure the

SHEPHERD WITH A ROD TO LEAD AND PROTECT THE SHEEP

flock. Dusk provides an invitation to predators. Consequently, daytime sustenance must be coupled with nighttime security. During biblical times shepherds had to defend their flocks regularly against wolves, but also, as David recalls, lions and bears on the prowl (1 Sam. 17:34–35). Today the Bedouin complain most of hyenas that kill several animals before settling down to devour one. It is only because of the shepherd's vigilance that the flock can eat "in the presence of my enemies."

The psalm ends (23:6) with God's "sheep" pursued by "goodness and love," returning to dwell at home in peace with his divine Shepherd forever.

THE DIVINE SHEPHERD IN THE WILDERNESS

The imagery of Psalm 23 resonates with accounts of God's pastoral leadership during Israel's wilderness sojourn.

> *He struck down all the firstborn of Egypt,*
> *the firstfruits of manhood in the tents of Ham.*
> *But he brought his people out like a flock;*
> *he led them like sheep through the wilderness.*
> *He guided them safely, so they were unafraid;*
> *but the sea engulfed their enemies.*
> *And so he brought them to the border of his holy land,*
> *to the hill country his right hand had taken.*
> *He drove out nations before them*
> *and allotted their lands to them as an inheritance;*
> *he settled the tribes of Israel in their homes. (Ps. 78:51–55)*

God rescued Israel from abusive taskmasters in Egypt, then supplied his people with manna, water, and quail so that they "lacked nothing" in the wilderness (Deut. 2:7). Their strong Shepherd spread a table before their enemies whom he had defeated (Ps. 78:19). God guided them through the desert by a pillar of fire at night and a cloud by day (providing also warmth and shade). He gave them his Torah ("teaching") as permanent "right paths." The journey led them to God's "holy pasture," the Promised Land, a place of "rest." There God made a covenant with his people and promised them long life (Ex. 15:13; Deut. 32:47).

After Israel lived unfaithfully for centuries in the Promised Land, God would, like a shepherd, "drive" his people into exile

Master of the Gathering of the Manna (fl.1460-75)/Musee de la Chartreuse. Douai, France/Giraudon/The Bridgeman Art Library

GOD RESCUED ISRAEL AND THEN SUPPLIED HIS PEOPLE
WITH MANNA IN THE WILDERNESS

to relearn the lessons of the wilderness. Jeremiah predicted the
Shepherd's recalling his people as a loving bride who "followed
me through the wilderness." He pronounced judgment on the
abusive undershepherds who terrified and scattered the flock.
The divine Shepherd vowed to regather his people and enter
afresh into covenant with them (see Deut. 4:27; Ezek. 11:9; Jer.
2:2; 23:1–4; 31:8–12).

   Like Jeremiah, Ezekiel pictured God's flock scattered on the
hillsides of the known world, suffering a judgment similar to
ancestors who rebelled in the wilderness (Ezek. 20:36–37). In
chapter 34, the prophet denounced the self-serving leaders of
the exiled community:

> *This is what the Sovereign Lord says: Woe to you shepherds of Israel who only take care of yourselves! Should not shepherds take care of the flock? You eat the curds, clothe yourselves with the wool and slaughter the choice animals, but you do not take care of the flock. You have not strengthened the weak or healed the sick or bound up the injured. You have not brought back the strays or searched for the lost. You have ruled them harshly and brutally. So they were scattered because there was no shepherd, and when they were scattered they became food for all the wild animals. My sheep wandered over all the mountains and on every high hill. They were scattered over the whole earth, and no one searched or looked for them. (Ezek. 34:2 – 6)*

God's pastoral passion for his people electrified this indictment. Anxious, leaderless sheep scatter. Without adequate attention, they become prey for prowling predators.

On the mountainsides neglect becomes abuse.

The Shepherd's unrelenting dedication to his flock prompts a string of promises for personal involvement and return to the pastures of Israel. Listen to the passion and resolve:

> *For this is what the Sovereign Lord says: I myself will search for my sheep and look after them. As a shepherd looks after his scattered flock when he is with them, so will I look after my sheep. I will rescue them from all the places where they were scattered on a day of clouds and darkness. I will bring them out from the nations and gather them from the countries, and I will bring them into their own land. I will pasture them on the mountains of Israel, in the ravines and in all the settlements in the land. I will tend them in a good pasture, and the mountain heights of Israel will be their grazing land. There they will lie down in good grazing land, and there they will feed in a rich pasture on the mountains of Israel. I myself will tend my sheep and have them lie down, declares the Sovereign Lord. I will search for the lost and bring back the strays. I will bind up the injured and strengthen the weak. (Ezek. 34:11 – 16, emphasis added)*

The Shepherd's heart breaks over the abuse of his flock in the hands of negligent undershepherds.

Isaiah predicted a similar "second exodus." God would once again free his people from captivity, shower them with miraculous provisions in a transformed desert, and lead them on a "way" in the wilderness by a glory cloud and his word, filling them with joy. We find more language of shepherding in chapter 40:

*See, the Sovereign L*ORD *comes with power,*
  and he rules with a mighty arm. . . .
He tends his flock like a shepherd:
  He gathers the lambs in his arms
and carries them close to his heart;
  he gently leads those that have young. (Isa. 40:10 – 11)[20]

THE GOOD SHEPHERD

In many ways Jesus' ministry resembled that of prophets such as Jeremiah and Ezekiel. He lampooned the leadership of his day and predicted the destruction of the temple. He saw the community as "sheep without a shepherd" who were "harassed and helpless" (Matt. 9:36) and in need of his pastoral compassion (Mark 6:34). With images reminiscent of Ezekiel 34, Jesus told the parable of a lost sheep to explain his ministry. In Luke 15 this story, bundled with stories of a lost coin and a lost son, highlighted his mission to "seek and to save the lost" (Luke 19:10). The Shepherd's care for the flock of Israel is expanded in Luke to include "tax collectors and sinners" (Luke 15:1; cf. Matt. 9:10), with whom he ate without condemnation.

John 10, the parable of the good Shepherd, further fleshes out Jesus' identity. He promised to show the full extent of his love for the flock by dying for them. In the shepherd parable

Todd Bolen/www.BiblePlaces.com

THE LORD GATHERS THE LAMBS IN HIS ARMS.

Christ affirmed John's declaration by saying, "I am the good shepherd. The good shepherd lays down his life for the sheep" (John 10:11; cf. vv. 15, 17, 18).[21]

Prior to these statements, Jesus depicted in this famous parable his relationship to his flock and the threats to their safety. His descriptions of thieves and wolves expose the religious leaders who were plotting his murder.

> Very truly I tell you Pharisees, anyone who does not enter the sheep pen by the gate, but climbs in by some other way, is a thief and a robber. The one who enters by the gate is the shepherd of the sheep. The gatekeeper opens the gate for him, and the sheep listen to his voice. He calls his own sheep by name and leads them out. When he has brought out all his own, he goes on ahead of them, and his sheep follow him because they know his voice. But they will never follow a stranger; in fact, they will run away from him because they do not recognize a stranger's voice. . . .
>
> Very truly I tell you, I am the gate for the sheep. All who have come before me are thieves and robbers, but the sheep have not listened to them. I am the gate; whoever enters through me will be saved. They will come in and go out, and find pasture. The thief comes only to steal and kill and destroy; I have come that they may have life, and have it to the full. (John 10:1–10)

Much of what Jesus describes here is understandable in light of traditional practices among Bedouin shepherds today. Jesus pictured for his hearers a pen that may have been an extension of a natural enclosure such as a cave or a crude, fenced-in area of stones or brush. The gate was not so much a door as an opening. Shepherds would have slept in that opening to protect the only entrance and exit to the pen. A Yemenite shepherd named Zacharia showed me a gate he constructed to protect his flock while he slept inside his house. He had suffered the loss of his flock to thieves three times, once losing over two hundred sheep.

The practice of sheep-stealing was common in the ancient world, as it is today. In fact, in some cultures, to steal a neighbor's sheep is an initiation rite for young men to prove that they are capable shepherds! In the parable, the thieves and robbers climb over the walls to steal the sheep, hoping to snatch those within easy reach. To thwart such theft, shepherds might have topped the pen's walls with briars, thorns, or small rocks that

THE ENTRANCE TO A SHEEPFOLD. JESUS CALLS HIMSELF THE
GATE: ANYONE WHO ENTERS THROUGH HIM WILL BE SAVED.

would make noise. The sheep's only real protection was the presence of the shepherd. Zacharia's new gate will never be an adequate substitute for himself.

Jesus likened the religious leaders not only to thieves and robbers, but also to wolves. Having interviewed numerous Bedouin, I have never found one without wolf stories. Prowling in the desert shadows, these predators take advantage of the vulnerable. Sometimes shepherds will put collars with metal teeth on their guard dogs because wolves attack the throats of their canine cousins along with the sheep. God's people are always at risk for wolves "in sheep's clothing" (Matt. 7:15).

Jesus contrasted himself with strangers who, like thieves, robbers, wolves, and hired hands, are not known by their flock. His sheep "listen to his voice" (John 10:3) and follow him because they "know his voice" (v. 4). Every shepherd has his own call or whistle to which his flock responds. Even when several flocks amass in an open valley, the shepherds can call their flocks, and the animals almost magically separate to follow their leader's call.

In the parable of John 10, Jesus reinforces the basis for his disciples' loyalty to him: his intimacy (knowing), his

CHAPTER SIX, THE DIVINE SHEPHERD AND HIS FLOCK   119

SHEEP KNOW THE SOUND OF THEIR OWNER'S VOICE.

protection (the gate, the sacrifice), and his intention to "save" them (v. 9) and provide "life . . . to the full" (v. 10).

GOD'S UNDERSHEPHERDS

John's gospel ends with a pointed question from the resurrected Shepherd, rephrased three times to Peter: "Do you love me?" (John 21:15–17). After each question, Peter affirmed his affection for the one whom he denied three times. Jesus responded each time with commands to feed and care for his sheep (vv. 15–17). The good Shepherd was transferring his work on earth to those for whom he had modeled self-sacrificing courage and compassionate provision. They were to continue following him—even to their own deaths (v. 19)—becoming like him as shepherds and as sheep among wolves (Matt. 10:16).

In Peter's first letter he seems still aware of this calling. Appealing to fellow elders he encourages them:

To the elders among you, I appeal as a fellow elder and a witness of Christ's sufferings who also will share in the glory to be revealed: Be shepherds of God's flock that is under your care, watching over them — not because you must, but because you are willing, as God wants you to be; not pursuing dishonest gain, but eager to serve; not lording it over those entrusted to you, but being examples to the flock. And when the Chief Shepherd appears, you will receive the crown of glory that will never fade away. (1 Pet. 5:1–4)

Later in chapter 5 Peter warns the elders to be alert because their enemy "the devil prowls around like a roaring lion looking for someone to devour" (1 Pet. 5:8).

The identity of church leaders as shepherds was important in the early church. In Paul's letter to the Ephesians he writes that the gifts Christ gave to the church are its "apostles . . . prophets . . . evangelists . . . *pastors* [shepherds] and teachers" (Eph 4:11, emphasis added). Later he encouraged the elders of Ephesus to "be *shepherds* of the church of God, which he bought with his own blood," warning them to be on guard for the inevitable prospect of wolves among the flock. "Even from your own number," he ominously predicted, "men will arise and distort the truth in order to draw away disciples after them" (Acts 20:28–30).

THE SHEPHERD-LAMB

The book of Revelation brings this image of God to a stunning crescendo. The only one worthy to break the seal and open the scroll is "a Lamb, looking as if it had been slain, standing in

IN MATTHEW, JESUS REFERS TO HIS PEOPLE
AS SHEEP AMONG WOLVES.

the center of the throne" (Rev 5:6). This Lamb will lead the survivors of the great tribulation, those who have "washed their robes and made them white in the blood of the Lamb" (7:14). The divine Shepherd will "shelter them with his presence" (7:15; lit., "spread his tent over them") and provide for them in a perpetual wilderness paradise.

> *Never again will they hunger;*
> *never again will they thirst.*
> *The sun will not beat down on them,*
> *nor any scorching heat.*
> *For the Lamb at the center of the throne*
> *will be their shepherd;*
> *he will lead them to springs of living water.*
> *And God will wipe away every tear from their eyes.*
> *(Rev 7:16–17)*

This picture beautifully summarizes the role of the Shepherd-Lamb; furthermore, it shows the decisive end to which all the wilderness experiences of God's people have pointed. God brought them into literal and figurative deserts to teach them dependence on their Shepherd (Deut. 8:2–5). The unique relationship forged between God and his people in these environments was perpetually reinvigorated in the Festival of Tabernacles—a celebration that all along anticipated heaven's pastoral paradise.

FAITH AND THE DIVINE SHEPHERD

Psalm 23 has helped to console countless souls. But, as we have seen, the Bible has much more to say about the divine Shepherd and about us as sheep and undershepherds. If the "shepherd psalm," as tradition tells us, was written by David, then it reinforces the important leadership lesson that we are all sheep before we are shepherds. As the good Shepherd, God provides for us, protects us, and guides us before we ever shepherd others. When our own compassion, courage, and wisdom run dry, we can turn to the God who "will neither slumber nor sleep" (Ps. 121:4).

Most shepherd imagery in Scripture is used to criticize poor leadership. The gravest mistake leaders can make is to forget who the true Shepherd is, the One whom we are called to follow. Pride spreads among those who forget that they answer to the Owner of the flock.

In one of my more memorable encounters among Jordanian Bedouin, I asked Abu-Jamal what it would take for me to become a

A SHEPHERD WITH A TRUE HEART FOR HIS ANIMALS.

shepherd. He said, "What really matters is if you have the heart for it. If you do, then you can begin tomorrow." He then surprised me by stating that his own sons would not inherit the family flocks; they didn't have the heart. In moments like these I could hear someone speaking in Arabic and another translating into English, and it seemed as if God was speaking to me. I could hear a divine voice saying, "I will give you shepherds after my own heart, who will lead you with knowledge and understanding" (Jer. 3:15).

Chapter 7

THE DIVINE PATRON AND HIS HOUSEHOLD

OUR EXPERIENCE of family life molds our view of the world and our place in it. For some, this experience has had tragic consequences. Many perpetuate a succession of abuse and cruelty, having known nothing different at home. Others become positive, contributing members of their community because they were given security and a sense of significance from their earliest age at home.

While the institution of family is a global reality, evident in every culture, the structures and meaning of family life vary widely. What comes to your mind when you hear "family," "father," or "sister"? As an American, I think of myself in terms of a nuclear family that sits at the intersection of two unrelated families. My travels in other parts of the world have caused me to realize how unusual this arrangement is. Unlike individualistic Western societies, most traditional, communitarian cultures are grounded in a *kinship* system, with the extended family, not the individual, as the basic unit. These societies are typically *patriarchal* (with authority vested in the oldest living male) and *patrilocal* (relatives on the male side live in the same location).

A JEWISH MAN HOLDS HIS SON WHILE HE PRAYS.
Geoff Manasse/PhotoDisc/Getty Images

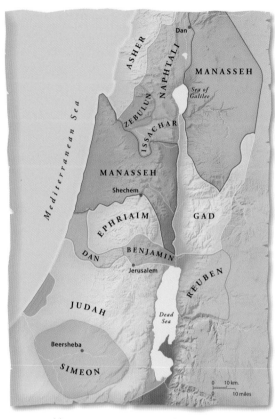

MAP OF THE TWELVE TRIBES

In kin-based communities a person's identity, status, and responsibilities are determined by the family whose genealogy extends back in history through ancestors with shared bloodlines. A preference for male lineage makes these cultures *patrilineal*. Larger society is experienced as a web of extended families. Intermarriage reinforces common bloodlines at the level of clan, tribe, and nation. For this reason, the Bible—reflecting the norms of traditional culture—is full of references to patrilineal family trees. Even though early Israel's twelve tribes were absorbed into a monarchy, the resilience of ancient family/clan/tribal identity returns centuries later in the genealogies of Jesus and in the images of the heavenly (tribal) congregation in Revelation.

While political realities reshaped their institutions in various ways, God's people have always been, fundamentally, his extended family. This identity has enormous ramifications for how we understand God the Father, how we treat each other as sisters and brothers, and how we engage with people outside the family.

MORE THAN A FATHER

In the ancient world a family was defined and identified by its paternal "head" (1 Chron. 8–9). Known sometimes as "patriarch" in Old Testament times or as *pater familias* in the Roman setting of the New Testament, the father was the patron of his household, the lord of his extended family. Patronage is a well-established system in traditional societies, one that provides clear expectations for all family members in relation to their head. "Household codes," whether formal or informal, determined the proper behavior for wives, children, and slaves in the context of an extended family (1 Peter 2:18 – 3:8). A patron might oversee three generations in his household (Gen. 46:26).

The terms *household* and *family* are not exact synonyms. "Household" adds spatial and economic dimensions to familial relationships. It implies a sense of place, with rich connotations that point to the space in which the family lives and works. It typically includes a family business, often supported by clients, stewards, and slaves. The patron assumes both rights and responsibilities with respect to the household that bears his name.

Because the ancients believed that the head of the family was its source of life, continued authority over that life became an institutionalized corollary. The exercise of paternal authority could be extreme. As the stories of the binding of Isaac (Gen. 22) and the vow of Jephthah (Judg. 11) illustrate, a father

Z. Radovan/www.BibleLandPictures.com

HOUSEHOLDS OFTEN HAD A FAMILY BUSINESS WHICH INCLUDED CLIENTS, STEWARDS, AND SLAVES.

THE SACRIFICE OF ISAAC BY CARAVAGGIO (1571–1610).
THE BINDING OF ISAAC SHOWS A RARE INSTANCE WHERE A
FATHER MIGHT TAKE THE LIFE OF HIS OWN CHILD.

in Old Testament times might, under certain circumstances, take the life of his own child.

The same was true in the New Testament period. Sources tell us that Romans placed newborns at the feet of the *pater familias* so that he could decide whether the infant should live or die. Children were often abandoned in the Roman Empire, especially infants whose value was compromised by gender or deformity. "The lawgiver of the Romans gave virtually full power to the father over his son, even during his whole life, whether he thought proper to imprison him, to scourge him . . . to keep him at work in the fields, or to put him to death. . . . He even allowed him to sell his son, without concerning himself whether this permission was compatible with natural affection."[22]

However, to be a family head was to bear a sacred duty, not simply a position of privilege and power. A father in antiquity was responsible for the provision, protection, education, and reputation of his extended family. This was especially important in Jewish culture, where the traditional view of the father as family priest and teacher was grounded in the Torah (Deut. 6:4–9).

In biblical cultures family responsibility was tied to family honor. Through generosity—whether as provider at home or benefactor in the public square — a patron maintained or enhanced the reputation of his family. This reputation could be tarnished by the misbehavior of children (Prov. 10:1; 17:21) or an unfaithful wife (Ezek. 16; Hos. 1–3). Everyone participated in the upkeep of the family honor.

The community's ideals were often personified in good fathers, who were examples of virtue, wisdom, and generosity both at home and in the larger community. Elders in such societies are drawn from the pool of model patrons.

SONS AND SIBLINGS

Children growing up in a traditional kinship system learn early and often that they owe their support to the family's economy and their complete loyalty to the household, regardless of its fate. Consider again some nearsightedness that may keep us from appreciating the cultural fabric of biblical stories. While Westerners have found in the stories of Joseph an example of moral purity and patience in trial, African readers recognize him as the epitome of a faithful son. At the end of

JOSEPH TAKING CARE OF HIS FAMILY DURING THE FAMINE.

kable life Joseph had managed to keep his father and
e, secured their material well-being, and chosen
idarity with his brothers over revenge. His final request was
that his bones be carried back to the land of his honored ancestors and buried in its soil. Our African brothers and sisters
accurately perceive Joseph's virtue as an expression of family
loyalty and faith in God.

One of the unquestioned responsibilities of siblings in
Israelite society was their fair treatment of, and absolute loyalty
to, each other. Though biblical narratives are full of dysfunc-
tional family misbehavior, the laws are uniform: love for one's
"brother" is required of all who share the same "father." (As
we will see, these terms are significantly elastic.) The Hebrew
word for "brother(s)" (ʾāḥ) occurs more than six hundred times
in the Old Testament, first appearing in the story of Cain and
Abel. It echoes seven times in Genesis 4:1 – 12, pounding into
the ears of the hearer the unavoidable responsibility of being
my "brother's keeper." This role is inescapably central in the
laws that followed.

As with fatherhood, responsibilities and rights defined
sonship. The story of the prodigal son illustrates the legal
entitlement that comes through birth — even to the unappre-
ciative. In biblical times, the firstborn son had double rights to
inherit the family estate upon the father's death. Israel possessed this favored status in a metaphorical sense. God judged
Pharaoh because "Israel is my firstborn son, and I told you, 'Let
my son go, so he may worship me.' But you refused to let him
go; so I will kill your firstborn son" (Ex. 4:22 – 23). The other-
wise inalienable rights of the firstborn could be traded away, as
we read in the tragic decision of Esau.

Though the imagery we are discussing is grounded in a
patriarchal culture, it has theological relevance to both women
and men. The biblical teaching of "sonship" is all the more rich
when we realize that what was once true only for firstborn males
is now true spiritually for all of us, male and female alike.

CHILDREN OF ABRAHAM

The genealogies that punctuate the book of Genesis (and many
other biblical books) illustrate how important *bloodline* is for

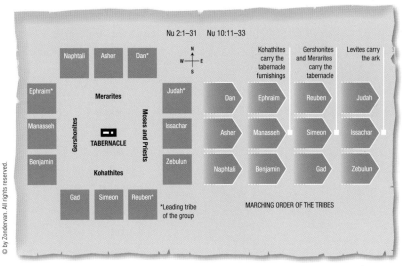

The following labels appear in the diagram:

Nu 2:1–31   Nu 10:11–33

Naphtali   Asher   Dan*

Ephraim*   Merarites

Manasseh   Gershonites   Moses and Priests   TABERNACLE   Judah*

Benjamin   Kohathites   Issachar

Gad   Simeon   Reuben*   Zebulun

N W E S

*Leading tribe of the group

Kohathites carry the tabernacle furnishings

Gershonites and Merarites carry the tabernacle

Levites carry the ark

Dan   Ephraim   Reuben   Judah

Asher   Manasseh   Simeon   Issachar

Naphtali   Benjamin   Gad   Zebulun

MARCHING ORDER OF THE TRIBES

THE KIN-BASED TRIBES ENCAMPED AROUND THE TABERNACLE.

the *story line* of Scripture. Before and after the flood two distinct family lineages appeared, one with favor and one without. Like Adam, Abraham stands at the beginning of a new line. God called him to do something radical: to leave his father, family, home, and, with these, his inheritance. Combined with this call, God promised him descendents (among them kings) as numerous as the stars, blessings, and land, which would be the family's inheritance. God deliberately waited until Sarah was beyond childbearing age to birth this new family and nation.

Genesis concludes with the survival of this chosen family through its promise-bearing sons: Isaac, Jacob (Israel), and the twelve sons of Israel. Exodus opens with a multitude of descendents (called, lit., the "sons of Israel" 750 times in Scripture) threatening Egypt, and it ends with a twelve-tribe confederacy camping at the foot of Mount Sinai. There God presented them with a charter, or "covenant," for life together in the land of inheritance. Having assembled in their kin-based groups for travel, worship, and warfare, they one day settled on their territorial allotments.

The Sinai covenant contains guidelines that reinforce the community's familial nature. At the Feast of Firstfruits Israelites were to affirm, "[Our] father was a wandering Aramean" (Deut. 26:5), thereby reaffirming a direct lineage to their forefather Jacob, whom God renamed "Israel." Countrymen were

TORAH SCROLL |

called "brothers" in laws that extended family behavior to the whole nation. For example, in Deuteronomy 22 the people were instructed to take responsibility for returning their "brother's" lost ox or sheep—*even if you don't know who your brother is!* (see Deut. 22:2 ESV). By contrast, some laws required family members to be cut off from the community if they were unfaithful to God—even "your very own brother, or your son or daughter, or the wife you love" (Deut 13:6–9).

What emerges in the Torah—which can be translated "teaching" as well as "law"—is a perspective of Abraham's family that is not synonymous with his physical bloodline. In fact, it was a "mixed multitude" that had left Egypt, including both Jews and Gentiles (Ex. 12:38 NASB). God was creating a family-nation that was circumcised in heart, not just circumcised in flesh (see Deut. 10:16; 30:6).

Moses' summary of the covenant community's true identity in Deuteronomy precedes the conquest of the Promised Land in Joshua. It could hardly be more significant that during their first battle in Jericho God excluded a native Israelite family (Achan's) and included a native Canaanite family (Rahab's). Here, at the beginning of their centuries-long stay in the Promised Land, God taught them what determined "insiders" from "outsiders." Not all of those who shared the seed of Abraham participated in his inheritance.

The stories of Ruth, a Moabite woman, and Jonah, who went to the Ninevites, reinforce this vision of an inclusive community. When Israel lost its land and freedom, prophets emerged with words of hope—even to outsiders who would have a place in God's family (Isa. 60:3; Jer. 3:17; Zech. 2:11; 8:22–23; 14:16).

Standing on Old Testament precedent John the Baptist minimized the importance of lineage, declaring that God could turn stones into children of Abraham (Luke 3:8). Jesus critiqued the self-inflated perception of some of these natural descendents of Abraham when he told his religious accusers

THE STORY OF ZACCHAEUS DEMONSTRATES HOW JESUS REDEFINED "INSIDERS" AND "OUTSIDERS."

that their real father was the devil (John 8:33–44)! Both John and Jesus perceived that "family resemblance" carried more weight than blood. Jesus demonstrated this throughout his ministry by dining with "outsiders" and calling a chief tax collector "a son of Abraham" (Luke 19:9). Abraham is the *spiritual* father of all who receive their family inheritance by faith (Heb. 11:8–19). That inheritance is available to anyone.

ABBA AND THE FAMILY OF GOD

The identity of physical and spiritual descendents of Abraham begs the larger biblical question of who the children of *God* are. The image of our divine Father runs deep in the currents of Scripture. Moses reminded Israel that God was "the Rock, who fathered you," yet you "forgot the God who gave you birth" (Deut. 32:18). Through Hosea the Lord said, "When Israel was a child, I loved him" (Hos. 11:1). In a graphic parable of Israel's rebellion, the prophet Ezekiel described Israel as an abandoned newborn daughter, left bloody in an open field by the Gentile nations (Ezek. 16). Yahweh cradled this helpless child as his own, clothing her and lavishing her with ointments and jewelry. The God of the Bible is pictured as a good patron, a loving father who has compassion on all his children (Ps. 103:13).

God's fatherhood is given full attention in the Gospels. Jesus routinely referred to God as "my Father," "the Father," and, in the Lord's Prayer, "our Father." In John's gospel, forms of the word "son" appear more than fifty times and "father" 136 times. These references carry a particular meaning for Jesus, the "Son of God," but they extended to the disciples. As Mary clung to her resurrected Lord, he told her, "Do not hold on to me. . . . Go instead to *my brothers* and tell them, 'I am ascending to *my Father and your Father*'" (John 20:17, emphasis added). He was going back to his "Father's house . . . to prepare a place" for them (John 14:2–3). Jesus welcomed the disciples into the intimacy and familial security of the love he shared with the Father. Believers have received "the Spirit . . . [who] brought about your adoption to sonship. And by him we cry, "*Abba*, Father" (Rom. 8:15). *Abba* is an Aramaic term that suggests legitimate access and secure intimacy.

Jesus' radical agenda reconstituted God's family. As God had done with Abraham, Jesus called men *and* women to leave their natural parents and siblings and all the traditional rights of family inheritance. To empha-

GOD'S FAMILY IS A DIVERSE GROUP OF PEOPLE THAT ARE CALLED TO GROW, LEARN, AND SHARE TOGETHER.

size the countercultural meaning of this new loyalty, Jesus called disciples to "hate" (meaning to "love less") their natural families as they joined his supernatural, spiritual family (Luke 14:26). Jesus encouraged his disciples to release their worries because he knows the needs of his own. If human parents are generous with their children, "*how much more* will your Father in heaven give good gifts to those who ask him" (Matt. 7:11, emphasis added). To these faithful few Jesus promised plentiful resources, an eternal inheritance, and a whole new family of brothers and sisters (Mark 10:29–30).

ADOPTION AND THE HOUSEHOLD OF GOD

The concept of adoption becomes an important key to understanding the nature of God's family. As important as the purity of the family "seed" was in antiquity, exceptions were made for adoption, especially during the time of the New Testament. Some evidence suggests that, technically, all children—including biological ones—had to be adopted before becoming fully enfranchised family members. Fathers in the Roman Empire had the authority not only to dispose of children they considered worthless, but also to grant the rights of sonship to those they deemed worthy of inclusion in the family.

Surrogate or "fictive kinship" was perpetuated at every layer of ancient society, from nomadic tribes to the imperial court itself. Five consecutive Roman emperors legally adopted their successors during the time of the New Testament. This not only reinforced a common social institution but also perpetuated "divine ancestry." The words of John's gospel take on special significance in this cultural context. "Yet to *all* who did receive him . . . he gave the *right* to become *children of God*" (John 1:12, emphasis added).

Adoption and fictive kinship were important features in a biblical household. Remember that a household consisted of an extended family living and working together under the leadership of its patron. Children—especially sons—were valued as junior partners in the family business and as an insurance policy for times of hardship and old age. The family's "clients"—servants, stewards, resident aliens, and other dependents—often became peripheral members of an extended family, contributing to the economic well-being of the whole. Some were formally given the family name to solidify their association, making fictive kinship an important feature of family life. Family rights and responsibilities accrued to those whom the patron selected to serve him and benefit from his support.

To put it theologically, family membership was fundamentally a matter of *covenant*.

Just as kin-based households were the

Wikimedia Commons

BUST OF EMPEROR TRAJAN WHO RULED FROM AD 98-117. HE WAS ONE IN A LINE OF FIVE CONSECUTIVE EMPERORS THAT LEGALLY ADOPTED THEIR SUCCESSORS.

FINDING THE LOST IMAGES OF GOD

building blocks of ancient Israelite society (collectively called the "house of Israel"), they later became the central units for the emerging church in the book of Acts (Acts 2:46; 16:14 – 15). Paul explained to believers how they should conduct themselves in "God's household, which is the church of the living God" (1 Tim. 3:15).

Adoption into God's household bore profound theological importance in the New Testament in light of the *ethnic* rift between Jewish and Gentile believers. Building on the inclusive vision that Jesus had lived out, Paul argued that while the Jews have a religious birthright by blood, Gentiles can receive the full rights of sonship through adoption. "Consequently, you are no longer foreigners and strangers, but . . . *members of [God's] household*" (Eph. 2:19). Gentiles (like Rahab and Ruth and most of us) become "heirs together with Israel" and "sharers together in the promise" (Eph. 3:6).

THE FAMILY ETHIC FOR ALL

Family loyalty in kinship cultures shields a household from the "out-group." The inclusion of ethnic outsiders in Scripture's new family ethic is dramatically countercultural. Jesus referred to those who do the Father's will as "my mother and my brothers" (Matt. 12:48 – 50). Earlier in Matthew he defined the Father's will as love for *all* whom God loves — even our enemies: "Love your enemies and pray for those who persecute you, *that you may be children of your Father in heaven*" (Matt. 5:44 – 45, emphasis added). As sons and daughters, we must resemble our Patron (John 13:35). John wrote, "Whoever claims to love God yet hates a brother or sister is a liar" (1 John 4:20). If we love others, we honor the Father (Rom. 15:5 – 7). *His* reputation is at risk in how *we* reflect *his* values. In the first centuries of the church, "the brotherhood" was known for the radical ways they served the poor, sick, and imprisoned, whether they were Christians or not (see Gal. 2:10).

John described one of the most noteworthy displays of solidarity among Christian siblings — the sharing of economic resources. "If anyone has material possessions and sees a brother or sister in need but has no pity on them, how can the love of God be in that person?" (1 John 3:17). Sharing was a

IN THE FIRST CENTURIES OF THE CHURCH,
CHRISTIANS SERVED THE POOR, SICK, AND
IMPRISONED AS IF THEY WERE FAMILY.

common *family* practice among the earliest church members
(Acts 2:44–45). One of Christianity's early critics ridiculed
the "poor wretches" whose "first lawgiver persuaded them
that they are all brothers of one another after they have trans-
gressed once for all by denying the Greek gods and by worship-
ping the crucified sophist himself and living under his laws.
Therefore they despise all things indiscriminately and consider them common property."[23]

Paul used sibling language more than one hundred times
in his letters to encourage unity (1 Cor. 12–14), sharing of
resources (2 Cor. 8–9), restoration of brothers or sisters who
stumble or backslide (Rom. 14:20–21; Gal. 6:1–2), greet-
ing with a "holy kiss" (1 Thess. 5:26), and even the freedom of
slaves (Philemon).

FAITH AND THE DIVINE PATRON

I learned a great deal about Middle Eastern hospitality from a
family in Bethlehem. Their son, Munír, became a good friend
of mine during a year's study in the 1980s. We shared meals
together with his extended family in their stone homes along
the town's outer valleys. They lavished boundless generosity
on me whenever I visited. Munír later came to visit my wife

and me in the States when we were directing a home for international students. As he entered the five-story brownstone in Boston, Munír quickly found himself immersed in an animated Arabic conversation with Walíd, one of our Jordanian students. After some persistent probing about the conversation, Munír explained that Walíd had extended to him standard gestures of Arab hospitality. He offered him food, cash, the use of a car . . . *anything that he might need* while he stayed at our house. He finished with, *"Whatever I have is yours."*

I was stunned and embarrassed. Here I was trying to be a good host to my brother in Christ, and a complete stranger offered more than I had — because of a remarkable yet simple sense of ethnic solidarity.

How I wish that our Christian family could find it this natural to extend limitless generosity to our brothers and sisters, *even to those we don't even know!*

NOTES

1. W. W. Hallo & K. L. Younger, *Context of Scripture* (Leiden: Brill, 2000), 2:426.
2. Ex. 25:6; 27:20; 35:8, 14 [2x], 28; 39:37.
3. Ex. 13:21–22; 24:15–18; 1 Kings 8:10–12.
4. 1 Cor. 14:3, 5, 12, 26; Eph. 4:12.
5. See also Jer. 7:31. After Josiah put an end to this practice during Jeremiah's ministry, this valley became the city's primary refuse dump. The corpses and ashes of people and animals were hauled there. Known for perpetual impurity and burning, Gehenna (Heb. for Hinnom Valley) would become a picture of hell itself (Matt. 10:28).
6. Think of Paul's words in Rom. 1:23: They "exchanged the glory of the immortal God for images made to look like a mortal human being and birds and animals and reptiles."
7. "Eikōn" is the Greek translation of the Hebrew term for *image* used in Gen. 1:26–27 and elsewhere for idolatrous images (Deut. 4:16; Isa. 40:19–20).
8. In Ezekiel's vision of a new temple he refers to the first human in priestly adornment (Ezek. 28:13), failing to protect God's precious "sanctuary" (vv. 16, 18).
9. The first word for my "loved one" (*dôd*) is the term used frequently for the lover in the Song of Songs.
10. The uncommon word for delight here (*ša^{ca}šû^{c}îm*) is also found in Prov. 8:30–31 for the feeling that personified Wisdom felt at God's side during the creation of the world. We have already seen human delight in the garden poems of the Song of Songs.
11. In the Greek version of Jeremiah 2:21 God says he planted Israel as a *"true vine."*
12. The Greek word means "to lift up" as well as "take away." Middle Eastern farmers often place rocks under their crawling vines to keep clusters of grapes from resting on the soil and rotting. However, Jesus doesn't seem to refer to this practice because he describes branches that "bear no fruit" here in verse 2 and later references in verse 6 to branches that are thrown away.
13. James B. Pritchard, ed., *Ancient Near Eastern Texts Relating to the Old Testament* (3rd ed.; Princeton, NJ: Princeton Univ. Press, 1969), 164.
14. W. W. Hallo and K. L. Younger, *The Context of Scripture* (Leiden: Brill, 1997), 1:397.
15. These phrases are virtually synonymous.

16. Throughout the Gospels the typical word for exorcism is the military term *ekballō* ("to drive out"), rather than other standard terms.

17. Eusebius, *Church History* 7.17.

18. See, in order, Isa. 11:5; 59:17; 52:7; 21:5; 49:2.

19. For more detail on these encounters and biblical insight into spiritual shepherding, see Timothy S. Laniak, *While Shepherds Watch Their Flocks: Forty Daily Reflections on Biblical Leadership* (Charlotte: Shepherdleader, 2007).

20. See also Isa. 40:3, 5 [cf. Ex. 40:34 – 38], 9 [cf. Ex. 15]; 42:4; 43:20; 46:2 – 4; also Ex. 6:6; 15:13.

21. Note how earlier in John, Jesus is compared to the "Lamb of God" who was sacrificed to "[take] away the sin of the world!" (John 1:29).

22. This quote by Dionysius of Halicarnassus is quoted by Andrew D. Clarke, *Serve the Community of the Church* (Grand Rapids: Eerdmans, 2000), 87.

23. Lucian of Samosata (*The Passing of Peregrinus* 13) from the second century, as quoted in J. H. Hellerman, *The Ancient Church as Family* (Minneapolis: Fortress, 2001), 128.

Share Your Thoughts

With the Author: Your comments will be forwarded to the author when you send them to *zauthor@zondervan.com*.

With Zondervan: Submit your review of this book by writing to *zreview@zondervan.com*.

Free Online Resources at

www.zondervan.com

Zondervan AuthorTracker: Be notified whenever your favorite authors publish new books, go on tour, or post an update about what's happening in their lives at www.zondervan.com/authortracker.

Daily Bible Verses and Devotions: Enrich your life with daily Bible verses or devotions that help you start every morning focused on God. Visit www.zondervan.com/newsletters.

Free Email Publications: Sign up for newsletters on Christian living, academic resources, church ministry, fiction, children's resources, and more. Visit www.zondervan.com/newsletters.

Zondervan Bible Search: Find and compare Bible passages in a variety of translations at www.zondervanbiblesearch.com.

Other Benefits: Register to receive online benefits like coupons and special offers, or to participate in research.

ZONDERVAN®

ZONDERVAN.com/
AUTHORTRACKER
follow your favorite authors